Relational Reality

Relational Reality

10 Ancient Secrets to Profound and Dynamic Relationships

LE Bailey Boydston

RESOURCE *Publications* • Eugene, Oregon

RELATIONAL REALITY
10 Ancient Secrets to Profound and Dynamic Relationships

Copyright © 2019 LE Bailey Boydston. All rights reserved. Except for brief quotations in critical publications or reviews, no part of this book may be reproduced in any manner without prior written permission from the publisher. Write: Permissions, Wipf and Stock Publishers, 199 W. 8th Ave., Suite 3, Eugene, OR 97401.

Resource Publications
An Imprint of Wipf and Stock Publishers
199 W. 8th Ave., Suite 3
Eugene, OR 97401

www.wipfandstock.com

PAPERBACK ISBN: 978-1-5326-7394-8
HARDCOVER ISBN: 978-1-5326-7395-5
EBOOK ISBN: 978-1-5326-7396-2

Manufactured in the U.S.A.   JANUARY 9, 2019

All Bible quotations are taken from the New American Standard Bible®, Copyright © 1960, 1962, 1963, 1968, 1971, 1972, 1973, 1975, 1977, 1995 by The Lockman Foundation. Used by permission.

Contents

Preface | vii

INTRODUCTION | 1

CHAPTER 1 | 6

    Something cannot come from nothing: there is a Creator

CHAPTER 2 | 15

    Diversions from #1 have very negative results.

CHAPTER 3 | 20

    Diminishing objective truth erodes intellect.

CHAPTER 4 | 29

    The paramount need for setting aside one day a week for relational reality.

CHAPTER 5 | 34

    Living humbly with gratitude under parental authority is foundational to healthy relationships.

CHAPTER 6 | 41

    We each are unique reflections of the Creator; relational restoration is always possible.

Chapter 7 | 47

Marriage of all human relationships is most unique.

Chapter 8 | 53

Love's evidence is creation; we are created to reflect the Creator; we are all creative.

Chapter 9 | 60

A life based in subjective fiction is no way to live.

Chapter 10 | 65

You are a unique creation; expressing your true self requires a connection to the Creator.

Chapter 11 | 69

The Creator's plan is empowerment for living in relational reality.

Chapter 12 | 75

Jesus came to make wrong relationships right.

Chapter 13 | 85

Spiritual reality

Chapter 14 | 90

Relational balance!

Chapter 15 | 94

The person of the Holy Spirit

Chapter 16 | 97

Good and evil

Conclusion | 101

Preface

I ONCE READ, "IF I ever had an original thought it died of loneliness." In the same way, I have no idea where many of the thoughts and ideas of this work came from, but rest assured most are not original with me. I have only added my unique perspective.

This book has taken a lifetime in writing. It is the expression of study and struggle. In this postmodernist America I think it will offend many; both Christian and not. It is my hope and prayer it will lead many to a new understanding of how to have loving, joy-filled, meaningful, lasting relationships based in an objective truth which lasts longer than time.

This book is not about external outcomes. It is about truths which transcend time when incorporated into one's life. They can internally change everything for good and thus impact those around you. It is about being right relationship with all: the Creator, people, animals, self, and even the environment.

This book is about life as it can be.

It is about life as it is meant to be.

Introduction

Relationships are a pain, no wait, a joy; they are without a doubt the greatest source of joy and pain in the human experience. Can't live with them, can't live without them! When we dwell on relationships, feelings abound; more often than not they fill our thoughts and crowd our emotions: marriages, dating, friendships, a close friend, maybe even your family, parent's siblings and all. Because countless different feelings and ideas come up when considering relationships, we each perceive them in unique and varied ways.

This is a blessing and a curse. Relationships are at the core of how we relate to everything. It determines how we relate to others and our environments. The ways we think about relationships define who we are.

At any given time every human relationship stands on uncertainty. At any given moment in any relationship, there are numerous questions to be weighed. Who really knows what motivates another? What makes them tick? What's motivating *you*? What dictates how you feel about something or someone? How can we be sure that the person standing or sitting across from us will be there tomorrow? Are they trustworthy, loyal, and dependable through thick and thin?

There is a way these questions can be answered, but only with serious thought with an open mind and heart. We must be analytical, making the natural progression of a relationship tricky. We never really know, if our relationships are based on another's emotional whim or the dynamic of honest committed life involvement. Without an objective standard we will ever be insecure, either on the brink of the insecurity of an explosive emotional passion with no lasting substance, or in continual confusion trying answer the challenge of understanding the another's motives and behavior. When looking at the world around us, it is even more uncertain. We live in a day and age where initiating relationships is easier than ever thanks to technological advances.

We as individuals and mankind stand on the brink. This is indeed the most unique time in history. Never in human history has there been such a time as this. Think about it: We all stand on the very knife edge of either the apocalypse of destruction or a utopia of astoundingly incredible potential. For the first time in history, three out of four individuals have some sort of influence thanks to mobile phones and social media. With an iPhone or good old wireless internet, you can have a worldwide impact!

On the destruction end of things, there is the ever-increasing threat of terrorist attacks, climate change, global nuclear instability, and the genuine possibility of global economic collapse. Scary stuff, indeed.

But on the astoundingly beautiful side is science and technology: artificial intelligence, wireless communications, space exploration like never before, the advancement of nanotechnology to enable the molecular biological repair of all biology. The latter means that we will soon have access to small biomachines in our bloodstream that can repair our bodies. There is even research in using nanotechnology with our crops with the potential of providing an endless food supply.

Based on these two polar opposites, a wonderfully fantastic future or destruction, there are a few predictions in both camps. One seems rather promising. If humanity does not kill itself or knock itself back into the seventh century within the next twenty-five years, the potential of human thought enhanced by artificial intelligence in conjunction with wireless communication and data storage solutions will be unlimited. So if you can imagine it, it

INTRODUCTION

will be possible to achieve it. Nothing will be out of the realm of possibility.

Of course, another prediction is not so bright: Military analysts and political experts tend to agree that at the rate many global tensions are evolving, we may face the threat of nuclear war (or horrors via other weapons of mass destruction) sooner rather than later. And it is this possible future outcome that makes most people take a good hard look at their lives—at the way they spend their time and how they value their relationships.

More than that, it raises a legitimate question of our own mortality. And that usually brings up the age-old question: *What is the point of being alive and self-aware?*

Why are we gifted with lives that can bring us fun and excitement in one breath, while doling out pain and sorrow with the next? And, perhaps more importantly, what can we do to better adjust to this reality? What can we do to make sure we make the most of our futures?

The truth of the matter is that the future is both terrifying and exciting in its potential. Take any two individuals, and they will likely give you a very different perspective on the future; those in good standing look at the future with hope and promise while those that are currently struggling with some of life's issues might see the future as nothing more than doom and gloom.

How the future will impact us—writer and reader alike—truly depends on all of us as individuals. The future depends on our courage to act on our knowledge and beliefs. Your passions and my passions, your morality and ethics and mine dictate our future. Our understanding of reality in our core being, our inner self-\, impacts and even governs every aspect of all our relationships.

Because of that, we have to give ourselves proper credit. You see, no matter who you are, what you think and believe *does* matter! We can no longer hide behind twentieth-century thinking that an individual is too small to matter or the comfort of believing our ethics and behavior are too small or isolated to have an impact over a larger reality.

So where do we start? Well, how about with a straightforward statement: *There is objective reality.*

A pretty simple fact, right?

It's as simple as the old adage that states, "Something cannot come from nothing." This statement, by the way, is also a simple and straightforward truth—a simple and straightforward reality. Nothing means *nothing.* It is the absence of all things. No light, no gravity, no time, no energy nor material. Nothingness means the absence of all. Logic and common sense dovetail at this point in simply understanding there has always existed the "cause without cause". From which all that is, has come from.

The act and theory of creation is another truth. So from this point on, to negate the point of nothingness, let's just agree to identify the source that abolished all of that nothingness by a name we are more than likely all familiar with: the Creator.

This is, after all, the name we humans give the cause without cause. This is the eternal source for all: the Creator—the intelligent, purposeful maker of the knowable and unknowable, the maker that exists both within and outside of time. A majestic and all-knowing Creator that waves together spring breezes and the interdimensional fabric all in one breath. And it was that same Creator that molded us to be thinking, emotional, and relational beings.

Short of the Creator himself (only using the masculine pronoun because it is the dominant pronoun in the English language), no one knows his true nature. It is only through his power that he made himself known to us. And in that revelation, it is up to us to use the gifts he provided—to use our basic logic and understanding to see if we can discover who he is.

It's quite tricky, of course. Even as believers, many of us often wrestle with how to fully grasp a Creator that has no beginning, but is responsible for creating us. It's this single point that serves as the crux of starting to understand the foundation upon which mankind's perception of reality and our opinion of life introduces our relationship with reality.

Introduction

But there are understandable questions that need to be answered. For instance, if we look at creation and/or ourselves, what should we look for as evidence of the Creator's mark or signature? Also, what clues do we have about the nature, temperament, and focus of what the Creator has revealed about his domain? Which of the things that he has created seem to be the most important to him?

To find the groundwork for these answers, we can start by looking at where the Creator invests his time and attention. There are ten principles given by the Creator. These principles are known throughout the world. The vast majority of people on the planet recognize them as foundational laws for human behavior but not as relational truths. Recognizing these historically proven and tested truths, we can see fundamental principles that he wants us to pay more attention to. And if we can find those areas, then we have also found a direction not only for how we are to live our lives but how we can successfully relate to those around us.

In his word, in his world, in his creation, he has left his mark. Those who create leave their mark on their creation. Those who create infuse their creations with their personhood and/or personality. I can listen to a guitar solo and identify Carlos Santana when I hear him. He invests himself in his art and creative playing. We too have been marked by our Creator, as the expression of the Creator's reality.

Now, what do we do with this information? How does this impact our daily lives? How do we live a life that is enjoyable and meaningful? Should it be defined by love, joy, peace, patience, goodness, gentleness, faithfulness, kindness, and self-control? Or should it be ruled by rigid rules of religion?

See . . . more and more questions. But fortunately, we have a Creator that has left us signs and guideposts. It's really no big mystery, though we do have clues to follow and evidence to discover.

Let's get started with the first clue: the very existence of the Creator and the resulting reality.

Chapter 1

There is a Creator who is beyond time, matter, and energy, who is in a relationship with his creation. This is the starting point for understanding relational reality.

ALL HEALTHY RELATIONSHIPS ARE based in and on objective truth or reality.

This reality is the inner truth or weight which keeps us centered in reality. This is the very core of reality, the very core of intellectual, emotional, physical and spiritual truth. We are creatures, not the Creator. We are made in the Creator's image, and thus each of us has a unique creative nature. The purpose of life is about discovering the Creator's image stamped in us as individuals and then reflecting that creativity.

When talking about relationships, it's a little difficult to not drift into subjective emotions and feelings. However, the best place to start when looking at the foundation of all relationships is this simple fact: *All healthy relationships are based in and around objective reality.*

Whether you believe in the Creator or not, you have certain core beliefs that help center you in your reality. These are beliefs that help you not view the world in your own unique way, but also likely shape your moral standing. However, for believers, it gets a little more fundamental. Our core beliefs come from Scripture and therefore shape our intellectual, emotional, physical, and spiritual

Chapter 1

truth. We are made in the Creator's image, and thus each of us has a unique creative nature. The purpose of life is about discovering the Creator's image uniquely in us as individuals and then reflecting that creativity.

Our thinking lives and behavior is based on faith—no matter if you are a believer, agnostic, or atheist. You act on faith when you sit down. You trust the chair will hold you and not fall. When you fall asleep at night you trust or have faith that you will awake.

In our relationships, we live in subjective faith in the other, and most conflicts occur when that faith is not justified or betrayed. You see, if there is no objective standard of reality or truth we are all doomed to a life of conflict brought about by subject faith based on sand or the whim of others.

Many people think science is objective and place their hope and faith in it. But science is wrong far more than it is right. Science is far to a shaky ground on which to build a life view. Just ask Galileo. The vast consensus of scientists of his day opposed his views, but he was right and suffered for it. Consensus is not science.

Let's take a look at more recent science which at the time was thought to absolutely correct.

THE NUCLEAR WINTER MISTAKE

In 1983, the famous astronomer Carl Sagan coauthored an article in *Science* magazine that shook the world. Titled "Nuclear Winter: Global Consequences of Multiple Nuclear Explosions," the article warned that nuclear war could send a giant cloud of dust into the atmosphere that would cover the globe. This cloud would block sunlight and invoke a climatic change similar to that which might have ended the existence of dinosaurs.

Skeptical atmospheric scientists argued that Sagan's model ignored a variety of factors, including the fact that the dust would have to reach the highest levels of the atmosphere not to be dissipated by rainfall. In a 1990 article in *Science*, a full seven years later, Sagan and his original coauthors admitted that their initial temperature estimates were wrong. They concluded that an all-out nuclear war could reduce average temperatures at most by 36 degrees Fahrenheit in northern climates. The chilling effect, in other words, would be more of a nuclear autumn.

It may seem like a minor blunder at best, but keep in mind that this is Carl Sagan we're talking about. Even if you don't buy into his every word or even his stellar reputation as one of the brightest minds of the last century, he put his name on the line when he published that article in '83. To come out and admit that he was wrong was huge for him. It also revealed to the public that sometimes even the brightest minds could get a few things wrong from time to time.

PILTDOWN CHICKEN

In 1999, a fossil smuggled out of China allegedly showed unmistakable proof of a dinosaur with birdlike plumage. The finding was initially trumpeted as the missing link that proved birds evolved from dinosaurs. It was displayed triumphantly at the National Geographic Society and written up in the society's November magazine.

Paleontologists were abuzz. So were small groups of the general public, as they saw something they had known to be correct about prehistoric history flipped on its head. Unfortunately, all of the hoopla was premature.

Just like a similar hominid skull with an ape jaw that had been discovered in the Piltdown quarries of England in 1912, the whole thing turned out to be a hoax. The fossil was apparently the flight of fancy of a Chinese farmer who had rigged together bird bits and a meat-eater's tail. Why he did it is anyone's guess. Fame, perhaps. Or maybe he just liked to play pranks on people.

He certainly did a good job. He not only fooled the public but some of the most noted experts in the field of paleontology.

CHAPTER 1

LIFE ON MARS . . . OR NOT

In 1996, scientists at NASA declared that a 6.3-ounce rock, broken off from a Mars meteorite discovered in Antarctica in 1984, contained flecks of chemical compounds—polycyclic aromatic hydrocarbons, magnetite, and iron sulfide—that suggested the existence of bacteria on the red planet 3.6 billion years ago. "August 7, 1996, could go down as one of the most important dates in human history," intoned one newspaper report.

But within two years the theory began to crack. Traces of amino acids found in the rock, crucial to life, were also found in the surrounding Antarctic ice. More damning, other non-Martian rocks—rocks from the moon, where it is clear life does not exist—showed the same "evidence" of life. By November 1998 an article in *Science* declared "most researchers agree that the case for life on Mars is shakier than ever."

Despite all of that, recent scientific methods and ambitious space programs are once again leaning towards the possibility that an ancient life of some form existed on Mars. There is even serious talk about water currently existing on the red planet in the form of ice and frozen sediment flows.

It seems, despite brilliant minds and billions of dollars, no one can quite make up their mind about what is taking place on your red neighbor.

FLAWED THINKING

Even the most genius minds get it wrong. Everyone makes mistakes. Just ask the scientists over at Space X, who know a thing or two about failures (just Google "failed rocket tests").

You and I make mistakes even when we feel that we are at our best and equipped with bright and "objective facts." People that rely on science for their answers and facts are often faced with the very troublesome notion that many accepted scientific facts and theories have a habit of constantly changing.

Relational Reality

You see, scientists get it wrong far more than they get it right, and when they do get it right, their findings are subject to change, given enough time and research. Discovering truth, or objective reality, is a noble goal. Finding such facts and explaining them so everyone who bumps into them sees them for what they are, not for what they want them to be, is virtually impossible.

Still, most humans do seem to have come to one general consensus: the most paramount aspect of reality is relational.

When we think of relationships, our emotions and feelings blur the lines of reality along with our subjective points of view. Where do we find the center point of truth and objective reality? For humans, relationships are everything. And we're not just talking about friendships and love interests. No, relationships can encompass just about everything that we have, one feeling or another. From the cute girl you crushed on in fifth grade to how we view the cosmos, it's all relational.

Think of how we understand the earth, or the universe, or laws of physics, time and space. And then compare that to our simple little understanding of our position as an individual within the structure of reality. It's a pretty broad spectrum—a spectrum that brings us to relational reality.

And what is the most basic and understood form of human relationship?

Love.

But, as we have seen, not all things we see as facts are always tried and true. So how can we view love in this relational context? How can we know for sure that love is real?

The primary evidence of love is creation.

And it starts with the very *gift* of creation . . . the extravagance of it all. Something cannot come from nothing. Nothing means nothing. No matter, no energy, no laws of physics, no universe, no multiverse . . . nothing.

Rational thought forces us to recognize we humans, of all creation, stand alone in rational thought. Something cannot come from nothing, therefore there has always been *something*. And that something created everything—us included. But we are the only

Chapter 1

part of creation which can intentionally reflect the image of that something—or the Creator. We exist as complex beings, capable of much. We were created in a way that allows us to exist on multiple planes: the physical, the mental, the emotional, and the spiritual.

As the Creator's image, we are created to reflect his image. We are *his* stewards of *his* creation. We are his stewards of one another. We are his stewards of the earth and all of life on its surface as well. In other words, I am my brother's keeper! Not to control, but to be a responsible honest reflection of the Creator.

Despite these responsibilities, we must always remember that no one is without their shortcomings. No one is perfect. Yet we all are accountable to live in reality and to reflect the reality we have been given to those around us. We each have a unique story that can be used as a direct and unique reflection of the Creator.

Just as most of the stars in the night sky are individual and unique, so are we. And while stars tend to get all the romantic notions and attention, we need to look to the moon if we want to see what we are supposed to be. The moon has no light of its own but is a simple a reflection of the sun's light and energy. In that same way, we too are a unique reflection of the Creator's reality, energy, and light. His creative nature exists beyond our physical death. His loving nature exists regardless of our individual shortfalls.

The ancients of old understood this truth, which has sadly been lost because of modern lines of thought which promote the idea of subjectivism—an opinion about reality that chooses to deny the objective truth that only nothing can come from nothing. Of course, such subjective thinking results in a severe misunderstanding of truth.

So what does this all tell us? Well, first and foremost, it shows that the first principle of establishing strong, healthy relationships is an intellectual understanding that there is a Creator; this Creator provides us with clear and simple truths which, when followed as he instructs, can result in a wonderfully creative, happy, and free life. Alternatively, when these instructions are not followed, the result can be devastating.

Relational Reality

As thinking and emotional beings, we want life to allow us to do whatever we want, whenever we want. There's nothing wrong with this on the surface. It's one of the things that makes us inherently human. We want the course of our lives to result in only positive consequences. In the face of relationships, this causes a problem because it leads to a rationale that believes my life and my choices need to dominate over all those I come in contact with. Mostly, if anyone has differing view or opinions, they instantly have conflicting desires to mine. This creates a winner/loser relationship, which is an automatic cue for failure.

And, of course, humans don't like to be controlled. So why would we wish such a thing upon ourselves?

As emotional beings, we find ourselves wanting to be the one in control. We want to manage and control all of the circumstances and environments that make up our lives. But since neither you nor I are the Creator of the reality in which those circumstances and environments exist, that simply can't happen.

This remains true despite the fact that humans are arguably the most significant reflection and evidence of the Creator. All of creation is a pale and meager study compared to who we are as living, creative beings—from our emotional drive to the very fundamental physical makeup of our bodies. That's right . . . the single most crucial evidence of a Creator is us. As a living, thinking, feeling, and discovering entities, we can't help but demonstrate the reality of a Creator. And this goes directly back into the first fundamental principle of understanding reality, the very foundation of all relationships: *There is a Creator.*

This is the starting point for a life of fulfillment, being who we are created to be, each of us as individual as a star in the night sky—each of us with unique abilities, skills, and relationships containing creative potential.

Unfortunately, societies have historically sought to replace this truth with subjective alternatives. These are alternatives that ultimately reveal themselves as empty, resulting in massive hurt with generational damage. When society thinks it knows better than the Creator, the results are miserable: slavery, wars, abuse of

Chapter 1

women and children, intolerance, gender confusion and on and on and on. These are the results of looking for an alternative truth rather than yielding to our Creator's reality.

Because of the relational reality of the Creator, he has given us the ability and nearly unprecedented opportunity to live a life of astounding love! The simplistic view of this is that we give our lives to him. In a relational sense, though, it requires action on our part; it requires a response to the reality he has created, our active pursuit of that love.

This type of life is one filled with joy, peace, and having the courage to do what is right regardless of our circumstances, environments, or subjective relationships. We are creative, relational beings at our core. We are meant to reflect a Creator who has placed the very spark of objective reality within us and a lifeline to himself.

In other words, picture yourself swimming in a lake, leaving little ripples and wakes behind you. Your relationships are not the entire lake, but just those ripples where you are passing through the water.

Yes, our lives and our relationships are ripples on a lake which are biggest close to us but continue to reach all the way to the shore. Even though when that ripple reaches the shore it is much diminished it still touches it. We rarely know everyone our lives touch and impact.

We are footprints on the shore of that lake, but not the entirety of the land.

We are essentially the butterflies in the scientific theory of the butterfly effect—a theory that states even the flutter of a butterfly's wings could have a lasting impact on the earth in some form or another. Even the smallest impact has a potential beyond measure.

So what will your effect be? Will it be based on relational reality or subjective wandering? How will you impact those you love the most? Will it be in truth and objective reality or in your own subjective hopes that are based on little else than wishful thinking and dream ideals?

Relational Reality

One leads to healthy permanent relationships and the other to nothing more solid or secure than a leaf wafting by on an autumn breeze. The choice, as they say, is up to you.

Chapter 2

Anything which distracts or diverts from objective relational reality with the Creator has resulting inherited and progressively negative consequences.

As we've already seen, even science can get it wrong. It's one thing to be wrong about a popular hypothesis or speculative theory, but quite another to be wrong about human physiology. Case in point: Before the completion of the Human Genome Project in 2003, scientists estimated that humans had around 100,000 genes and that complex species have the most genes.

It turns out, we actually have around 19,000–20,000 genes. We also discovered that a tiny moss plant has around 32,000 genes—making us puny humans realize that maybe we aren't the most complex organisms on the planet.

We humans are so subjective, so based on emotion and locked in our own paradigms, that it's impossible to sustain healthy relationships without an objective standard or a foundation in objective reality. Relational reality is dependent on personal and social integrity. Honesty with self and others is often a hard exercise. The whole field of psychoanalysis is built on helping folks be honest with themselves and building the skills to be honest with others.

Because we are the very reflection of the Creator, we are free to express ourselves in any way we choose. But if we do not recognize and yield to the reality of our Creator, we create a rip in the fabric of who we are and who we were created to be. The connection to objective reality is severed; as creative beings, we weave our own subjective fiction to answer our own questions and to fill the emptiness in our spirit. In our minds, we willfully begin to search for false answers, building a fiction we are comfortable with created by our own wants and comforts—regardless of what a healthy relationship with the Creator ought to be.

We are all a reflection of the Creator. You are uniquely a creative person. We are creative folks by nature, as such without an objective base we start to create alternatives to foundational relational reality. We begin to build relational systems and societies based not on objective reality but on subjective alternatives. These usually are alternatives with our very own standards and desires at the core. And then this can lead even farther down this dangerous path by setting us on a self-propelled course to finding any means to justify an acceptable substitute for the reality the Creator has designed for us.

When these substitutes are lauded as truth, we also skew what should be the most essential thing in life—the Creator himself. When this gets off the tracks, the results are chaotic and, quite frankly, dangerous. We get societies based on the principle of every man for himself. Everyone is looking out for Number One. And this obviously distorts the very fabric of what makes wholesome and healthy relationships. When we are too busy focusing on our needs and what we would like for our individual realities to look like, we lose sight of what healthy relationships should look like.

Think of it like this: Picture someone that has planned and planned for a trip out into the woods. Perhaps it's a hiking trip or a camping outing. They are venturing deep into the forest, so they have taken a compass. But the woods are familiar and there is a path, somewhat overgrown but still there. So this person decides that they don't need the compass after all. Yet, if you speak to anyone that has ever ventured into the forest with a specific location or purpose in mind, they will tell you that if their course is even just half of a degree off, they will never reach their destination.

They can, in fact, get hopelessly lost.

Chapter 2

Now, for a more harrowing example, let's step off of our imagined path in the forest. Consider that people that grow into adults and carry these misguided realities as truth also pass them down to their children. What we get as a result are entire generations that are living under subjective misdirection. But, as we know, what is lost can be found.

You see, the foundational principles of who we are and who we were created to be rest in our very DNA. The social part of our lives, the endowment of his character placed in each of us, still bubbles to the surface at one time or another. Love, joy, peace, patience, goodness, gentleness, faithfulness, kindness, self-control, righteousness, and wisdom are descriptions of the Creator's character invested in each of us. These are simple truths we learn from childhood in clever songs about the "fruit of the Spirit."

But when we ignore the reality he has created for us and opt for our own, these fundamental truths and principles can be compromised. It can create a generational erosion of the single most crucial aspect of healthy relationships. The apparent nature of the Creator that has been sewn into each of us becomes threadbare and can be torn.

And if that ultimate relationship can be damaged this way, just think of how it can effectively harm all of our other relationships—husbands, wives, family, friends, coworkers, and so on. We so quickly begin to seek subjective temporary distractions rather than permanent meaningful lives rooted in reality when something doesn't fit our fragile little created realities.

When we throw off reality, we live a life of fiction. We are writing our own little stories and we have set ourselves in the place of the main character around which the rest of the plot hinges. But then when the expected results of our fiction begin to fail us, we want a whole different story. We want to turn the page or skip a chapter. And as a result, those in whom we are invested start to sense a shift in us. That is, if they notice; after all, perhaps the other people in your life have fictions of their own too. Mix this all together and conflict is inevitable.

This can easily spread like cancer without anyone being aware of it. It spreads from a single individual to that individual's social groups, family, and so on. It can then spread to towns, political parties, tribes, entire nations. This has the ability to run so rampantly so quickly because those who have more skill or influence in any given area can dominate others either by force or example. And when this example is followed, we are separated from the Creator, using our own created truths with what the Creator intended.

You see, the fundamentals of human philosophy are amazingly consistent. There seems to be an underlying truth that people from every corner of the earth agree upon: that there is a common ground of sorts of fundamental morality. But that commonality can so quickly become shattered as people began to weave their own fictions and live by them as if they were the truth. It is the very definition of a vicious cycle.

This way of life and logic will become so commonplace and normalized that we will perceive these fictions as reality—that is, until someone else's fiction seems more compelling to us or when our own fiction has started to collapse because there was never any real foundation.

The sad thing in all of this is that all of these created fictions will one day ultimately collapse. Because without the design of the Creator, none of it has any real foundation. It harkens back to the parables of the wise man building his home on the rock while the fool built his with a foundation of sand.

Of course, the fool in the sand does not realize that he is a fool until his house starts to slip, slide, and crumble away.

Whether we are a Christian, Buddhist, or atheist, it is our duty to stand firm with objective truth. For those lost in subjective fiction, this firm standard seems harsh and unyielding, even as folks on a boat when looking at those on shore worry about running into the firm land. We can stand in truth and warn these people away from the subjective fiction of selfish design. But we must do it with understanding and love rather than judgment and the wagging of fingers. This is crucial because we are relational beings and even when we are at a disagreement, we have the need for

Chapter 2

a center point of relational reality which we all have in common. This is real no matter your belief, age, background, or culture. Even infants that cannot yet put together a cohesive thought can be severely affected developmentally if they are not held and loved.

Our relationships are where we have our greatest joys and sorrows. The people we love, our friends and family, make our lives meaningful. But if we place anything in between us as our own creators, leaving the true Creator out of the equation, it will negatively impact all of our relationships.

It is like trying to run a gasoline engine on diesel fuel. It is work briefly, but it always ends badly.

Imagine what your life would be like with a permanent connection to the one great truth of a Creator whose sole desire is the expansion of his love and wisdom in and through you. Not a mindless robot, nor a radical religious fanatic, but a genuinely emotionally healthy person grounded securely in objective reality. Free to be yourself, safe and secure enough to risk expressing yourself in your passion. Standing in absolutely honestly in who you are and knowing the absolute acceptance of the Creator's love and power.

This is objective relational reality! This is what all relationships should be founded on and what they should all strive to be.

Allowing distractions from the Creator's reality strips us from the sole anchor of his objective truth. His desire is for you as his creation to reflect his creative loving character to all: friends, family members, animals, plants, and the complete environment. We are his stewards. He is invested in us far more than we can know.

When you can begin to accept these things as true, it means that you are never far from the Creator. While you have been searching for your true self, he has known the true you all along!

It all begins with heartfelt internal prayer and humble gratitude towards the Creator—a yielding of self-will to his will for your life without reservation. That's all it takes to allow him to rebuild in you an objective relational reality that will last forever. We have everything to gain and nothing to lose. Be your objectively true self so that you do not have to live in a subjectively woven fiction any longer.

Let reality set you free!

Chapter 3

Treating the objective reality of the Creator causally results in the eroding of all relationships, intellect, and/or objectively clear thinking.

PICTURE THIS WITH ME:

A husband and wife, married for over thirty years, are walking down the street. There's no conversation, just the pleasure of each other's company. As they are strolling along, they happen to pass a beautiful young woman. As they pass, the young woman smiles at the couple. After a few steps the husband, with a smile on his face, says, "Honey did you see that beautiful young lady smile at me?"

"So what," his wife replies. "Remember the first time I saw you? I laughed out loud!"

This funny example demonstrates how folks in a relationship have very different subjective perceptions of the same event. The conversation could have gone a lot of different ways. Perhaps in another alternate version of this story, the wife responds in anger. Why would her husband of thirty years be interested in another woman or even care that another woman was smiling at him?

Or maybe the wife might even take a moment to appreciate the fact that, yes, her husband can still attract the attention of other women—making her either appreciate him more or even question her husband's devotion to her.

Chapter 3

The good thing about this example is that no matter which avenue the contrived plot takes, it all comes back to one fundamental principle: respect.

Even if it *was* evident that the young woman was smiling at the husband, he should not comment on it out of *respect* for his wife. But because he did, the wife is also faced with an issue of respect. And as we see, she deflected the comment with a snarky sort of sarcasm that seemed to be a good-natured joke. But even jokes can be tricky, a perilous road that can often lead away from respect.

Respect is so often a hinge point for our relationships. In tandem with the power of words, the absence or presence of respect in a relationship can make or break that relationship. Words, after all, are how we communicate the most effectively. Words carry meaning and reflect our respect of those to whom we are speaking.

Using our words is perhaps the single most powerful aspect of relational reality. We are told in Scripture that the Creator spoke and all that we have ever known, all that we currently know, and all that we will ever know came into existence. So when we speak, it has an impact—sometimes even permanent implications.

I'd feel like I wasted an opportunity here if I didn't share a saying that my grandmother always had at the ready: "Let all your words be sweet; you never know when you may have to eat them!"

This is true in all forms of speech. How we speak has an impact on others as well as ourselves. Words are how I place my thoughts, ideas, and even emotions in your mind. I believe that fear is the most significant cultural shortcoming in my lifetime. In our current day and age, we have started to treat language as if it is a necessary evil instead of the singularly most important aspect of civil society. With the modern era of smartphone texting, we are rapidly moving to emojis, memes, and GIFs as a lazy and somewhat restrictive way of utilizing language skills and thereby diminishing our ability to seriously express how we feel in words.

Popular language is on a continued downward spiral where some of the most revered artists and cultural icons are shamefully bereft of being able to speak without base references and relationally damaging utterances. Just look at popular music, at political debates, and even humorous movies or television shows. Humor has degraded into a shocking denigration of respected people and organizations focused on the most juvenile immature aspects of relationships. And sadly it is becoming an almost accepted norm in our culture.

This is dangerous, even when it is painted in a "joking" light. Speaking to someone with respect recognizes the Creator's reflection in that person. Talking to them absent of that respect does the opposite. And it can cause irreparable damage.

If you want to see the lasting effect of words, look no further than the development and needs of young children. I can personally think of several children I have met in my past who have been substantially damaged because of hurtful words used by a thoughtless parent. These words, even when spoken in passing out of frustration and anger, cling to children as they grow up. It can often lead them to feel worthless and unloved.

I can pretty much guarantee that there is not a single human being alive today that can't think back to at least one negative thing that was said about them (either to their face or behind their back) that didn't sting . . . that didn't stick with them and in some way alter the way they behave or carry themselves.

It is with our words and language that we either honor relational reality or speak so casually of our Creator that our words begin to erode our intellect. The truth of the matter is that we also use words to glorify him . . . or to present him as something merely secondary. The same words we use to tear down or lift up other people can be used to glorify the Creator and his reality or to water it down. When we do this, using words that aren't uplifting or praising, we begin to place barriers of doubt between our Creator and us. When we guard our speech as we speak of the Creator, it tempers all conversations with others—whether those conversations are expressly about the Creator or not. Because of this, we need to practice a mode of thinking before we speak that helps to set a pattern of thoughtfulness in our speech. In our current culture, we have gone so far from this truth that the importance of it has been all but lost. Even at the highest levels of government words are used casually with no understanding of their permanent impact on the hearts and minds of others. The ripples reach out and touch far more than intended. Words have a permanent impact for they express who we are.

It's quite clear that words have meaning. Not just between us, but when we refer to or about our Creator as well. Speaking casually or profanely of our Creator has a devastating impact! It diminishes the perception of his reality in those who hear and in the one talking. It creates a false narrative between our Creator and us. Speaking or behaving as if there is no relational objective reality may not appear to do damage to the truth, but it does! It's just that the loss seems ever so slight at first. And from there, it can become the foundation for genuine doubts not only in reality but in the Creator as well.

When this occurs, it moves individuals and society off of the solid foundation of truth—that truth being that we are created beings, not the Creator. Speaking casually of the Creator transmits a casual yet cascading contempt for truth. The results are a continuing downward spiral of social and relational developments.

Relational reality depends upon speech (communication) to place our thoughts, desires, affections, hopes, challenges, and emotions in another's mind. When we speak, we reveal, for the most part, a glimpse into who we truly are. We become transparent, or we mislead others about reality. When we choose to speak of the Creator in a way which creates doubt or diminishes the objective reality of the foundation of all relationships, we erode our most important relationships. It exposes the crack in our innermost being, a special place where the Creator should reside.

Over the years, I have noticed those who are the most profane are usually the same ones that tend to be bullies or those that are extremely careless in their relationships. Harsh language and a tendency towards biting sarcasm start to reveal inner selfishness. When this behavior is how we discuss or view the Creator, we are primarily relying on a subconscious method of elevating ourselves by calling on the ultimate arbiter of justice as if we control him.

Relational Reality

Our language reveals who we are and what we believe and think. It allows others and even the world to glimpse into our mind and heart. Even more critical, our words have the power to influence others for good or for evil. They point people in directions we are seldom aware.

As an example: I was told some time ago that a casual remark I made in the past has had such impact that it has helped form a direction in the person's life. I say only to give the most explicit example that I can personally share from my past. It also makes me wonder what other things I have said that stuck with people that I just don't know about. It's staggering to think about it, really.

Or here's another example—maybe you may be able to relate. This is a comment that was made to me that was not intended to hurt but stung enough to stick out in my mind some thirty-five years later. The comment in question was made thirty-five years ago while I was playing a game of ping-pong. While playing, someone I considered to be an excellent friend, one whom I greatly respected (and still do), offhandedly mentioned that he and "some very good friends" were going on a trip.

This stung at once because I had not been invited to go on this trip. I didn't even know anything about it. His casual remark bore no ill will towards me, nor was he even aware of the impact it had upon me. But it revealed his mind and heart. When unguarded, our speech can be a very profound thing. Even at the best, most guarded times, our language reveals our hearts and minds. To allow such a dominant aspect of who we are to be used without self-control is a dangerous thing.

When our language is simplistic, childish, careless, or profane, it communicates inherent laziness to grow beyond a limited vocabulary and willingness to accept a subjective standard based upon perceived peer acceptance. It demonstrates, for whatever reason, laziness of thought or a willingness to yield one's intellect to a demonstratively degraded social group.

If you want to see this in action really, just bring to mind that wise age-old saying: "What goes around comes around." This is not only true of degrading talk that tears other down; it can also

Chapter 3

be seen in the arena or rumors and gossip. Think about it . . . anything I say carelessly, no matter how innocent it might seem, has the potential to be heard and repeated elsewhere. This is especially true when you have the sponge-like ears of little children around.

When words get away from us, they can be harmful in so many ways. Rumors brew in the workplace, doing remarkable damage to a company or an employee. A careless or hateful word at school leaves lasting impressions upon children. One errant word between husband and wife can cause tension and arguments for days, weeks, or even longer.

So how do we stop this from happening? How can we put guards up against letting our words get away from us?

Well, self-discipline in our speech begins with a proper understanding of objective truth or reality. When starting to live in relational reality, we yield ourselves to the truth of the Creator as the actual standard. Our speech then begins to reflect our respect for that truth. When we start to live and speak out of respect of objective truth, it allows us to subjectively reflect reality to those we come into contact with. With intent, we move beyond the baser aspect of careless language and move into a thoughtful language which reflects respect to those with whom we are speaking.

When we speak to someone else, it is usually more than just casual chit-chat. In anything we communicate to someone else verbally, we are typically seeking to accomplish several things at once. These include but are certainly not limited to:

The desire to convey an idea or feeling

The desire to establish or end an ongoing relationship

The desire to discover or share information

The desire to purposefully misdirect another

In each of these examples, when we see the one to whom we are speaking as a reflection of the Creator's love and purpose, we must project our words with respect. To approach the communication with anything but respect (yes, even in the example of misdirecting someone) is to place both the speaker and the recipient in danger of being distracted from reality.

The language we choose is a reflection of our understanding of reality in a social context. Our selection and use of words reveal the priorities of our true selves. Even when we speak casually and without thought, our speech habits reflect those things in life we place the most value on. And here's the real kicker, where a lot of people tend to seriously struggle: the people we love the most certainly deserve the most respect from our speech, but those we may not particularly like so much need our spoken respect just as much. Whenever are are speaking to someone, we are speaking to a uniquely created, one of a kind, reflection of the Creator.

Of course, this sort of mindfulness towards how we speak takes discipline. We have to be able to recognize when our own thought patterns are being affected by the things others say as well as by the things we say to others.

My wife and I were recently on a tour of Winsor Castle in England. I was amazed by the respect and awe the British still hold the royal family. I was standing just outside the castle wall when I asked a jogger who had stepped out of the rain about the recent royal wedding. The jogger spoke with respect and awe. The royals, regardless of personal perspective, have an objective history established through hundreds if not thousands of years of acceptance that they are, by "God's" choice, the rulers of the land. To understand the truth of this does not matter if you believe it or not. It is that the jogger gave the "royals" the respect and honor as God's chosen! *You are God's chosen!* Whenever we speak to and/or of someone, we are talking of the Creator's elected person to reflect his image! Speaking to anyone with less than honor and respect is to disrespect the Creator.

When we hear the spoken word, even if we speak it ourselves, it reinforces what we learn. Guarding our words by developing a pattern of respectful speech to everyone we come in contact with begins with a clear understanding of objective reality. By placing a priority on living in reality, we are acknowledging the Creator and can begin reflecting his truth in our casual speech.

Chapter 3

I can think of no better example of a person deliberately developing a discipline of mind and speech than George Washington. As a young man, he created a list of specific attributes to live his life by. By age sixteen, Washington had written out by hand what was known as *110 Rules of Civility & Decent Behavior in Company and Conversation*. Some of them demonstrate how important language and respectful behavior are and are applicable even today. For example, consider these "rules" and how you could be putting them into practice in your own life:

Every action done in Company, ought to be with some sign of respect, to those that are present.

Sleep not when others speak, sit not when others stand, speak not when you should hold your peace, walk not on when others stop.

Shake not the head, feet, or legs, roll not the eyes, lift not one eyebrow higher than the other wry not the mouth, and bedew no man,s face with your spittle, by approaching too near him when you speak.

Turn not your back to others especially in speaking, jog not the table or desk on which another reads or writes, lean not upon anyone.

Show not yourself glad at the misfortune of another though he were your enemy.

Superfluous compliments and all affectation of ceremony are to be avoided, yet where due they are not to be neglected.

Speak not injurious words neither in jest nor earnest scoff at none although they give occasion.

Think before you speak, pronounce not imperfectly nor bring out your words too hastily but orderly and distinctly.

Use no reproachful language against anyone neither curse nor revile.

Boiled down and give a modern-day translation, these are rules that are relatively simple to follow. Imagine the impact as you practice these on those you love the most, maybe around the home. After all, as we have already discussed, speaking without honor or respect to those we love the most is precisely the opposite of the sort of language and actions which build loving, emotionally strong, thoughtful people. This applies even to sarcastic or flippant language within the homes that we often pass off as joking.

Always consider your words carefully at home. If the home is indeed where the heart is, the way we use our words there will say a lot about our hearts and how we view our homes.

Chapter 4

Set aside one day a week for building, reinforcing, and/or restoring relationships based on reality. Beginning with the Creator, then one's spouse, moving to children, then extended to family and friends, then spreading to the community. Without this weekly reinforcement of objective reality, subjectivism will erode all relationships.

COMMUNITY IN ALL OF its many forms is an integral part of relational reality. It's where relationships are formed and nurtured, where we get closer to those we love as well as with our Creator.

There is the adventuresome and romantic idea of the solitary man standing defiantly against nature or overwhelming odds, possessing nearly superhero-like qualities to overcome all obstacles to win the day. It is an experience that is quite often presented in fiction, mainly because it doesn't usually occur in reality.

Still, in the autobiography of Daniel Boone, the quintessential solitary man in America's frontier, he wrote that the worst time he ever had in the woods was when he was forced to remain in the wilderness by himself following an accident where one of his companions broke his leg. His brother, who was the third member of the hunting party, had to take the friend back to the village. Daniel had to stay and hunt by himself during the winter or his family and others depending on him would go hungry. He was by himself for several weeks in the cold, in the wilderness. And even this famously rugged man claimed that it was among the worst periods of his life. He wrote it was a great challenge of his life.

Men are not meant to live alone. The inner strength of a man is established by his connection to the Creator and nurtured by the context of relational reality, to his wife, family, friends, and community.

Without the accountability of community, people will drift towards selfishness and self-centeredness. And, as we've already seen, that can quickly lead to living for that fiction we have created for ourselves, a fake reality that tears us away from the Creator. However, when are regularly a part of the community, we find inspiration and encouragement from others, which paves the way for access the objective reality the Creator had designed for us.

All of our relationships must be healthy. Just as we must eat regularly to be healthy, we must also take on the day a week for living in reality. Setting aside the distractions of work and or self-motivated endeavors, Deuteronomy makes it pretty clear that we are to invest one day a week on abiding in relationship with the Creator, family, and friends.

Of course, it is so easy to become distracted by the world around us as we forget reality. We get caught up in the obvious and immediate. We can become engrossed in our work, studies, hobbies, leisure activities, and so on. And while there is nothing inherently wrong about any of these things, they can slowly start to tear away at our relationships and community. It's a slippery slope; a day or two of rest and relaxation just to focus on self-centered things that seem harmless can so easily hurt or emotionally disengage those that are closest to us. Without a habit of yielding our inner selves to the objective truths of the Creator, we all drift toward personal desire and preference in life with no more solid a foundation than what are often misdirected emotions, resulting in a subjective fiction which we begin to blur with objective reality.

Our own work and recreational or creative endeavors are basically where we invest ourselves in to receive rewards. Money and recognition establish a value on our time and energy—a value

Chapter 4

that is tangible, unlike the emotional benefits that come from the community. And with money and success we find another slippery slope: the more we get, the more we want.

When we build our lives around this mentality, we begin to create yet another fictional life around us. The fiction here is that by seeking money, success, and power we are essentially seating ourselves at the throne and becoming the "creator" of our own little warped reality. We begin to build a belief system build upon our fictions. And according to Deuteronomy it must be reset every seven days to bring us back to authentic reality. This is because the Creator is the center of all relationships and is able to give real balance to those relationships. In turn, it is our responsibility to reflect his character to those that we interact with.

The weekly reset reinforces his attributes of love, joy, peace, patience, goodness, kindness, patience, faithfulness, and self-control within us. The need to keep centered and well balanced is a need of all relationships we intend to keep healthy and happy.

This "reset day" is a day where we set aside the routines of our typical days to focus on the most important things of life: relationships. This is a day where we take the time to be with those we love and enjoy, and to appreciate not only them individually, but the relationships the Creator has fostered among us. This is the one day to lay aside stress, worry, distractions, and the anxieties which build in us as we live in a world with millions of individual fictions all around, vying for our attention.

Setting aside one day a week recharges our relational realities, and allows us to rearrange our priorities, placing those we love most above ourselves. These breaks will enable us to understand better and help each other to replace the growing subjective fictions of our lives with the objective reality of the Creator. When we take this break every seven days, we become transparent in our motives while helping those around us grow more confident in relational truth.

When we can quickly start to develop this kind of sustained relationship-building, the solidity of our friendships and family systems become so much stronger, as they are rooted into an idea of family and community that was intended by the Creator. When we forgo this approach for our own needs and fictional realities, most of our gathering times with friends and families tend to rotate around attendees' subjective agendas. Sure, there may be a common reason for gathering, but each person there has a priority based in subjectivity.

Yet with the accepted standard of the Creator, there is a center point of reality to which all issues and relationships can be set towards. By then setting aside our own agendas, these reasons for meeting with one another (hence, "community") can then be made symmetrical and aligned with the way the Creator originally intended. This standard which the Creator has given us creates a unique aspect of relationships. When we gather and seek genuine relationships beyond our own agendas mainly when gathered to celebrate or better understand the Creator and his rules for us, there is a dynamic which occurs. This dynamic bonds those within the group in a unique way, permanently molding them into a reflection of the Creator's intent.

For an extreme example of this, think of men that go into war zones or experience rigorous military training together. For many of these men, a special lasting bond takes place in these situations. And while I have never experienced this before, I *can* clearly remember my father—a career military man—sitting down with other military men that he had not seen in several years. When they got together, those years between them seemed not to exist; it was like they had seen each other just yesterday. More than that, it was almost as if they had *always* been a part of each other's lives.

When you get right down to it, when we gather in the name of the Creator, it is no less than a life-and-death struggle. But the gathering has to be genuine. It cannot be deluded with rituals or meaningless motions and empty recited prayers. We cannot let these meetings become formulaic and just something we do every week to check off a box.

There is real power in the community when we get together as a God-led group. When we gather in the name of the Creator, it is not just our lives that we are trying to enhance, but those that we maybe haven't even met yet.

We have the potential to lead lives where we follow our Creator's intent. But what, exactly, is the Creator's intention? What does any artist wish to express? Where does the creative spark come from? Where the home of creativity? Where is the source of that single unique leap in thought which starts an entirely new line of thinking or expression?

How did Einstein leap to relativity? How did Newton leap to modern mathematics? Where did Bach's music come from or Mozart's?

Any artist creates to bring something new into the world. And when we look at the magnificent work of our Creator, even in something like community and relationship-building, it's clear that while we are indeed his creation, we are a constant work-in-progress.

Chapter 5

Living humbly with gratitude under parental/honored authority is the foundational objectively internal truth which anchors to our reality and is the bridge from emotional/relational immaturity to healthy emotional/relational balance.

TO SET UP OUR next relational guideline, I'd like to take you on a stroll through a real-life example—an abridged story, if you will.

Judy is thirteen years old. She is pretty, smart, quick-witted, and has her pick of just about any of the boys in her school. But even at a young age, Judy has been sexualized to a remarkable degree. Her mother is a drug addict. To help pay for her habit, Judy's mother has been trading her for sex since Judy was nine years old.

In this situation, poor Judy really didn't have much choice. Her mother, whom she probably thought was looking out for her best interests, started her down this twisted path at such a young age. So what was she supposed to do? What choice did she have?

What we see here is a life sent on a traumatic course before the one living it really even had any say-so in it. How could Judy ever have a normal life or ever have any healthy relationship—not just with men, but women too? After all, how would she ever establish a sense of trust with another woman, particularly one with a level of authority over her?

Chapter 5

Now, while this is a radical example, the sad truth of the matter is that these stories are far too common. I know this from firsthand experience.

For many years, I severed as the executive director of a non-profit organization that worked with children with behavioral, mental, and emotional challenges. I have seen many of these heartbreaking stories. And this story of Judy I have shared with you is one such story (the name, of course, changed to protect the young woman's identity). And when I started to realize that these sorts of things were taking place not only in the world but in *my* part of the world, it was a game-changer for me.

But through this story I also got to witness a sort of rescue. I was blessed to watch as a great man equipped with the truth of relational reality stepped into Judy's life. This man saw Judy for who she really was: a handpicked reflection of the Creator's love for an abused individual. He saw in her the uniquely molded reflection of reality. He saw the potential for all of Judy's pain, hurt, and abuse to be overcome by love, joy, and peace. Through a nurturing relationship with the truths of the Creator at the core, the Creator through this man was able to rebuild an emotional foundation within Judy's heart.

But how does one go about doing this when so much damage has already been done? Where does someone begin in restoring a person? How do you start to build a healthy individual up when all they have known is hurt, deceit, and pain?

Well, thanks to Scripture and the work of the Creator, we can look back on historically proven truths for these answers. Finding such objective truths require us to go to the very foundations of human reality or the oldest written principles of relational reality for humanity. One of these is rather well-known to practically everyone: "Honor your father and mother."

Or, to be more specific: "Honor your father and your mother, as the Lord your God has commanded you, that your days may be prolonged and that it may go well with you on the land which the Lord your God gives you" (Deuteronomy 5:16).

Some of you might ask how a young woman like Judy would ever be able to do this. She has been betrayed by all she has ever known and trusted. How could she possibly honor her mother, father, or any parental authority?

It seems as if Judy is caught in a catch-22, wherein anything she does results in a bad outcome. But that is only a subject perspective. The objective reality is painful yet rewarding. Overcoming her circumstance required forgiving those who had abused and mistreated her. When we look into our own hearts and see our natural desire to be the very center of our own subjective reality, and see we have the same potential to hurt and damage others as we have been when we lack the connection to the Creator, it enables us to forgive the other. The healing secret was found in letting go of past abuses and relaxing in the truth of a Creator who has purpose and direction for every individual. It involved placing her trust in the objective reality of the Creator and learning to be the person he created her to be.

The man that eventually came into her life was able to lead Judy to relational truth and reality in her life. Through his help and starting a relationship with the Creator, Judy discovered a life of joy, peace, and security. Judy began a life of love and adventure by finding the Creator's reflection in her own heart. She is now reaching out in love and acceptance to others that are caught in the same web of abuse she has come out of.

In Judy's case, her old fictions were torn down, and her life was rebuilt in reality and restored in the only real method of restoration. Whether we are aware of it or not, we are all in need of repair. We have all faced the choices of deciding between right or wrong—and have often chosen wrong. We have all known the truth and the lie and elected to tell the lie.

We all desire to be the objective truth of our own lives as well as the lives of others. Unfortunately, we are not. The Creator is. There is objective truth and reality. There is a way to live in relational truth, and it begins in humble gratitude to the Creator—loving gratitude for our lives and his loving intent for us.

Chapter 5

The concept of being humble is often misunderstood. Humility could be defined self-control as strength caused by respect for another. It could also be interpreted as living for someone other than you, always putting your needs and desires last. Or, to put it today's terms, realizing that you really aren't all that. For example, think of parents that are living in a fictional reality, not humbling themselves before the Creator. Sure, they think they know what is best for their children, but when they are caught in their own fictions, the reality of objective truth can stunt a child's emotional growth. It can also result in a child's unintentional tendency towards swerving relationships of their own in the future just to meet the needs of their own subjective realities.

The internal draw to live as if our subjective points of view (our personal fictions) are paramount is overwhelming, and without constant reinforcement of objective truth, we will drift away. And it is the responsibility of our parents to clearly set us on his course. It is by a parental example of living in objective truth and striving to live a life based on the reality of the Creator that children learn a proper behavioral balance. Balanced parenting requires a clear understanding of the Creator's nature and intent for his creatures. His will for us is not a mystery, as some tend to say. He has created each of us to reflect his creative objective nature in our own unique subjective life. The further we are away from this reality, the more the fiction of subjective relationships develops. When he is replaced in our lives through intent or neglect, our relational attachment to reality drifts. And naturally, the sooner we start to realize this, the better—which is why the fundamental relationships between parents and children are so meaningful.

It is through loving direction and correction from the objective point of reality that children are under the authority of their parents. Parents have been tasked with guiding them into living a life based on the principles of the Creator's reality.

We have been created to live in relationship with him, reflecting his love to all and reproduce his nature through our creativity. We learn this from our parents and learn to live a life of reality rather than one of distracted emotional and relational turmoil.

When we as parents begin to live in our own fictions, we build a life of invention for our families and children—a fantasy where the lines of objective truth and subjective opinion are blurred. Teenagers are a great example of a precarious age where life without the Creator at their center may start to seem like a genuine threat. As teens, relationships revolve around how they feel on any given day. Sooner or later, objective reality sets in and the fiction upon which a life has been built is shown for what it is: a sad distraction.

Without the reliance upon objective truth, rebellion and self-centered fiction begin to rule the day as they search for meaning and truth in life. They are looking for an alternative to the reality that will serve them and them alone and will be pulled away from anything resembling real truth or humble gratitude towards the Creator.

Growing into adulthood with relational misalignment results in a life of doubt, questions, and uncertainty. Life meant to be lived in joy, love, and peace can quickly start to spin out of control because the control is in the wrong hands. The center of gravity (the Creator) is missing, allowing their lives and relationships to falter.

It's plain to see that children, teens, and adults alike all have one thing in common: All of their relationships are based in a searching dependence to fulfill the insecurities left open in the past by trying to live in a reality void of the objective reality of the Creator.

When the Creator's objective reality is the foundation in a relationship, the standard is created within that relationship. It is a standard upon which the trust within the relationship can rely on whenever conflicts or disputes arise.

In the picture of a parental relationship to a child, it is the actual relationship with the Creator *through the parents* that establishes unassailable parental authority. The parents are accountable to the Creator to reflect his image to their children to develop the security and foundation for their lives.

Being able to cast this reflection on children requires quite a bit of spiritual and emotional strength. Emotional strength—like any other strength—comes from exercising. But as in most

Chapter 5

exercises, you need a solid point of reference to react from. Push-ups, situps, and jumping jacks need a solid base for support. Pull-ups need a bar attached to a foundation. Running requires a path or road to follow. Gravity or objective relational reality keeps us anchored.

Similarly, growing emotional strength needs a solid foundation to push against. If the foundation is fixed and secure, the exercise is more comfortable. Yet if the foundation is subjective or fragile, you will quickly grow not to trust the platform on which you are exercising. You will find yourself continually making changes, learning to adjust your behavior with the unstable object with which you are using. And when you do this, you start to live your life as if your own subjective actions are more important than the foundation itself. And if we want to stick with the exercise metaphor, it's *this* action that causes you to injure yourself during a workout, or burn out, or just push yourself too hard.

Really, we've all experienced this in one way or another. We have all been deceived into thinking our own feelings are the most important ones. When we perceive that our "reality" is the only viable one, we enter into a life of subjective fiction. When we sense that we are the center of reality, we begin to disregard the truth. How we relate to reality or objective truth is the foundational basis of our emotional development.

There are nine benefits from a life infused with relational reality founded in the Creator; some of you may know them by another name: the Fruits of the Spirit. These nine benefits are love, joy, peace, patience, goodness, gentleness, kindness, faithfulness, and self-control.

These are qualities that are always present when you are living with the reality the Creator designed for us. They are not temperamental or fleeting, and they are not dependent upon the circumstances of life. These aspects for relational reality are emotions and behaviors that can be strengthened through exercising our emotions within the Creator's intent for life. When you can live by these qualities, and within that true reality, you will begin to understand better and identify the "true" you. This true you are a unique reflection of a loving Creator who has created you as just one aspect of his reality. And when you are a living, thriving part of this reality, your relationship with the Creator becomes more intimate than ever before.

Chapter 6

Individual relational restoration is always possible. Being the Creator's image, we have in ourselves the capacity to bring relational restoration vs. destruction. The old adage: "Treat others as you would like to be treated."

WE'VE BEEN QUOTING FROM Deuteronomy quite heavily, but I'm going to throw you a curve ball with this following quote.

> "The mind is its own place, and in itself can make a heaven of hell, a hell of heaven."
> "I am the master of my own fate; I am the captain of my soul."
> "Better to rule in hell than serve in Heaven."
>
> —John Milton, *Paradise Lost*

These words from Satan's mouth as penned by John Milton in *Paradise Lost* have found a home in the heart of modern thought—particularly in those that frame themselves as progressive thinkers. In truth, I am sympathetic to the idea myself. Deep down, I think we all are.

I would love to be almighty. I'd love to have the influence and power of the Creator or at least a superhero, a being with superpowers to control all circumstances and bend all things and everyone to my will. Who wouldn't want that?

Then I recall several great thinkers of the past and their thoughts on an unaccountable life. There have been those who have lived with no accountability for most of their lives. They had total power to control those beneath them with absolutely no penalty for bad behavior. Perhaps you have heard of a few of them: Adolf Hitler, Joseph Stalin, Pol Pot . . . to name a few.

There is an old saying you might know: "Power corrupts; absolute power corrupts absolutely." While we all want some degree of power, I am afraid of the kind of person I would become if I was completely powerful with no consequence. All people are flawed by self-centered priorities. When left only to our own opinions, passions, and devices we place self over all other things. Eventually, my self-centered ego would seek its own pleasure and desires at the expense of others—even those I love. I know it's true because it has happened. At times I have chosen self-centeredness at the expense and to the pain of those I love. Not because of any desire to do harm but out of sheer self-preservation. My guess is you have as well. It's part of being human. We all know a couple of things about each other. You and I both have known the truth and known the lie and chosen to tell the lie. We both, you and I, have known the right thing to do and the wrong, and chose to do the wrong. Yep, there it is, we abandoned objective truth and chose subjective fiction. I am afraid to look at how bad I would be without accountability.

If you look closely at Hitler, Stalin, and Pol Pot, they all started out with their view of what was good and what was right for themselves and the country they loved. And we know how it ended up for these individuals. It went terribly wrong because of a self-centered, subjective relational perspective. They lost objective truth to subjective fiction in which they created their own versions of good and evil. Evil was anything which did not conform to their subjective fiction. Therefore, they essentially placed themselves above the Creator and lived by their fiction while pressing it upon others.

These men are some glaring examples of how people with certain influence can use their fictions and false realities to mold and shape others. When this happens and our emotions and actions

Chapter 6

are held over others by a position of power, rank, or influence, we become designers and implementers of our own subjective fictions, thus replacing objective reality.

These are also men that seemed not to understand that were are but mere creatures. While we are created to some degree and like to think that we are unique in that creativity, we are not the Creator. We are free to express our individuality, our true selves as unique expressions of the Creator's reality. The choices we make concerning how we live are the expression or reflection of the Creator's sovereignty over not just us, but everything in existence.

When someone chooses to live outside of social norms and act purely out of self-interest at the expense—and sometimes the pain—of others, they become what society refers to as a criminal. And while we know that basic behaviors are what keep people from becoming criminals, there is actually a fine line between the two. After all, what makes a criminal? Most of us would agree that a crime comes about when someone disregards the agreed-upon set of rules and behaviors that keep society running safely.

But did you ever stop to think about where such a concept came from? It came from the very same ancient principles that we've been discussing. It came from the Creator's expression and intervention to instill in his creation a pattern of life based in objective reality—a reality reflecting his love and grace.

Of course, it's natural to wonder what it feels like to live by our own self-interests. It is natural to think that if we surrender our self-will, we will lose our free will to be who we want to be and to do what we want to do. But it is only when we begin to live in relational reality to the Creator that we really find out who we are. The security of living in authentic relationship to the one who designed us, infused his image upon us, loves us, and is focused on our best is the most freeing experience possible.

To live outside of our his will for our lives is to live a life of insecurity and not anchored to objective reality. This easily becomes a life which is dependent upon the whims of our social and physical environment—which, as we've discussed, is criminal as its core. This would be a life where we would live in a continual avoidance of reality, frustration, fear, and anger when life begins to spin out of our control.

Yet, life always spins out of control, doesn't it?

As I write this there are massive fires burning in Northern California. Multimillion dollar homes are being burned down. The fantastic wealth of the area is what most folks seem to aim for, yet it takes less than one fire-ravaged night for all of those wealthy possessions and objects of desire to disappear. Those flames can't be stopped by money, power, influence, or social and political positions. None of those things can stop reality. That's right . . . even the harsh edges of reality are the making of the Creator—which harkens to the age-old question about why bad things happen. Well, when bad things happen, this is when the Creator's reality can best be reflected.

Being anchored in reality can be harsh. Life sometimes hands us brutal consequences. Being a good person won't keep those consequences away. Being a good or an evil person has no effect upon the laws of nature. We are all treated the same. The Creator has given us the perfect environment to reflect his nature and character. He has also given us an environment, a world, where massive harm, hurt, and destruction are not only possible but likely. We have to remember that we live in a fallen world that Scripture tells us "groans like a mother during childbirth."

Perhaps a bit unnaturally, living in relational reality is most profound when bad things happen. The worse the event, the greater our potential to show our amazing reflection of the one in whose image we are created. The greatest reflection of the Creator is self-sacrifice. And courage is measured to some degree in self-sacrifice. For instance, when a firefighter runs into a fire when everything in his body and mind is telling him to run away, he is choosing to rescue someone else over his own self-preservation. Or when a police offer puts himself in the line of fire between a criminal and a potential victim, we see this same level of self-sacrifice.

So . . . if our own individual realities—subject fiction—were what we lived for, and my own perspective of life and my environment are the only "true" things, what is the point of it all? Would

Chapter 6

there be any need for courage or self-sacrificial acts if there was no true objective reality?

If life is only about "my reality," meaning that what is genuinely true is only my perspective of life and environment, if life is only an accident of time and material, why risk it? What's the point? Many would try and argue that the need to act in courageous ways in order to preserve the species is just an inherent nature to survive. But these are the same folks that would argue that mankind, as a species, is destroying the earth and that humans are the single greatest threat to the natural order of things.

In their subject point of view, these people miss reality. Objective reality at times of greatest stress often breaks into personal reality. Self-sacrifice is the single greatest reflection of the Creator—an image we see exemplified in Christ dying on the cross. For within the complete understanding of this kind of risk-and-reward analysis, there is no easy-to-observe self-reward. There is nothing selfish about such an act, no benefit in place for the one putting themselves at risk. While there may be an argument for sacrificing yourself for your child or another family member providing a benefit to you, the act itself can still be seen as courageous.

When our lives are based on objective reality, we have a foundation for our emotions and behavior. Without this objective relational reality for a basis, the subjective aspect of who we are sooner or later always dominates. Without this fundamental ingredient of life, we would all become wrapped in self-centeredness, seeking to bring others under our control. When we are grounded in relational reality, we have the strength of character to give of ourselves without fear of losing ourselves.

In other words, we begin to understand and experience transcendent love—placing another before ourselves, without losing ourselves in the process. In fact, this is the opposite of the perspective of those who talk about their "personal realities." You see, by giving ourselves away in this form, we discover who the Creator designed us to be. Love is the expression of life (or consciousness). It is truly the only thing which exists that works opposite of and may govern the physical laws of the universe.

As odd as it may sound, the more you give away, the more you have to give. The truth of this is even now being verified in your heart and mind. The Creator has gifted all people with this amazing aspect of his nature and it displays the most fundamental aspect of his nature: love.

Creation is the evidence and the product of love. This is true in our biology and in human experience. When we love someone or something, we tend to become creative. In the case of loving another person, we get creative on how to please them, how to keep them happy. In the case of loving our environment, we work hard to keep it clean and thriving.

This is the hope for humankind. This is the hope we have when we live in relational reality. Our loving Creator created us in his image to love as creatively unique individuals, expressing who we genuinely are made to be.

Chapter 7

Fidelity is the reflection of the Creator in all relationships/ marriage. Marriage above all human relationships is most unique. It is the most reflective of the Creator's nature. Where a man and a woman come together as one, bodies are complementary, emotions are complementary, and mental perspective become enhanced.

I'D LIKE FOR YOU to think of some great injustice from your childhood. Perhaps a sibling was able to stay up later than you. Or maybe your best friend got all the latest toys while you were stuck with hand-me-downs. And in these situations as a child, what was your go-to argument for such injustices? For most, it's three simple words: "That's not fair!"

Whether or not we want to admit it, it's a phrase we at least think to ourselves off and on as adults. But have you ever stopped to wonder why we go there? More to the point, what definition of "fair" are we using when we make this statement? Where, exactly, does our sense of fairness come from?

Whenever we say or think "That's not fair," we are assuming that the sense of fairness exists and that we are appealing to some higher power or judge which will arbitrate your subjectivity against objective reality. After all, who or what are you making such a statement to now that you're grown up and there are more than toys are bedtimes at stake?

We tend to resort to a sense of "ought." That is, "Things ought not to be this way" or "Things ought to be different." But again, where does this sense of ought to be come from? And really, it all boils down to the basic core of an objective standard—a standard that reaches all the way back to the Creator.

Relational reality is genuinely expressed by love with the resulting creative results each of us is stamped with. As individuals, we are a unique reflection of the Creator, yet there is a limitation in our finite reflection of the Creator's actual nature. The Creator transcends individuality in the same way he transcends time and space. As scripture and countless ancient writings tell us, one of the most amazing aspects of his nature is love; the very social nature of the Creator's essence is love. It is evident in Creation itself, as well as in the self-sacrificing nature we have already discussed in sending Christ to the cross for the empowerment to reach relational reality for all mankind. What this shows us is that his omnipotence and authority over all things cannot exist apart from that other part of his being—genuine love, right at the core of it all. As such, even as we as individuals are created in his image, there is an aspect to his nature which requires another!

We are told in the oldest of ancient literature that we were created, both male and female, in the Creator's image. So only by the coming together of male and female is there an accurate reflection of the Creator. This allows us to glean that there is an aspect to the Creator which signifies the coming together of male and female in a committed preference to the other. Not just to be together for one another, but also to honor and respect the other, to seek the other's betterment at all personal cost.

Today, we see this in marriage. Marriage is the temporal reflection of the very nature of the Creator. What this means is that your marriage is more than just the union of man and wife, but a reflection of the Creator to the world. Not just his image—it is the very expression of his core being. Marriage should consist of a love

Chapter 7

so absorbed in the other that it prefers the other over self, resulting in creative expansion of reality.

Marriage is perhaps the best representation of his transcendent nature. Neither male nor female alone is sufficient to exemplify this. It takes both together to create a bond transcending individuality without negating it. There is a joy in marriage which transcends any and all other relationships on earth, and that joy comes from giving yourself away to another selflessly without reservation.

If your goal in life together is to have a great relationship then the single tried and true path is to put the other first. The husband is to put the wife first in all things and the wife is to put the husband first in all things. In marriage, when you give yourself away without a reservation, then you find your true self. Marriage is perhaps the safest and most secure environment in life in which we can practice true self-development. As partners in the give and take of life, the ups and downs of emotions, the joys and heartaches that come to us all, we begin to develop a maturity which allows us to pass on this joy as truly loving parents. After all, marriage is the foundation block for emotionally healthy, secure children.

When you give someone your love, it is theirs to do with as they please. It is your gift to them. And marriage is the one place in our lives where that gift can truly be cherished and kept safe.

In today's society, the word marriage raises a lot of definitions and questions. So let's take a look at it in the way the Creator refers to it. Given the Creator's set of standards, marriage is defined as:

Two inherently (biologically) different people coming together with the blending of their minds, emotions, and bodies, giving oneself to another without reservation or cost; this results in their love becoming so substantial and whole that they become "one"—essentially a new person.

Seems pretty cut and dried, right? Well, there is and has been throughout the ages an absence of relational or objective reality. In the twenty-first century, there has been a pattern of thinking which is based on subjective fiction. This thinking is based on a desire to be inclusive at all cost. The goal so far in the twenty-first century seems to be a headlong rush into unfettered thinking disregarding physical and intellectual facts. Subjective fiction at its most obvious.

The best example is the idea of a personal preference of self-gender selection obscuring the rational thinking which reinforces biological fallacy. This has created a subjective fiction which not only suggests but also promotes many genders beyond the reality of two genders: male and female. Yet historically there has been a very small subset of people who through no fault of their own are biological anomalies that are confused as to the objective truth or relational reality. In an effort to justify themselves in the mainstream of reality, they promote a perspective that is a deviation from reality; it is neither mainstream nor objective truth. And even though the two genders are backed not only by our Creator but science as well, the current popular mainstream line of thought sees any such truth as condemnation rather than reality.

The Creator's expressed attitude toward of this kind of subjective fiction is love and forgiveness with a desire for all to be properly aligned to objective reality through an acceptance of reality and his forgiveness of the personal deviation from reality. As such, those that live in accordance with the Creator and his reality should approach such deception with humility and gratefulness for his love and guidance.

When you look at the fundamentals of marriage, the core of the comparison comes down to the two distinct sexes. There really is no good agreed-upon scientific explanation for sex within the theory of evolution. One of the more current explanations and theories states that having two distinct sexes rather than one universal sex cuts an organism's reproductive possibilities in half. However, this is the system that has persisted in nearly every species on earth. No one is quite sure for the reasoning behind this, although there are a few theories. For example, some think that two sexes, male and female, are less likely to breed with family members than one sex, and therefore create stronger offspring. Other theories on the rise of two sexes include the Hurst-Hamilton Hypothesis, which talks about how the mutational dynamics of the

Chapter 7

mitochondrial genome would have favored the evolution of sexual reproduction. Whatever the reason for creating two sexes, it seems to work and is likely here to stay as the main way new life emerges.

Surrendering to this kind subjective reality is to fall into creating a false narrative as to the very nature and reality of the Creator. It creates a fiction which leads to billions of subjective fictions and confusion about reality.

We've already briefly discussed how the highest and perhaps noblest behavior in relational reality is when a selfless act enhances another. Marriage, as the Creator intended, is the absolute best illustration of this. As a woman and man give themselves to each other without reservation, the bond which take place elevates them both. They are elevated physically in some cases, spiritually in most cases, and emotionally in all cases—when marriage is conducted in a way that is synchronized with the Creator's relational reality.

Most of the great truths of life are simple. More importantly, they are relational. Oddly, though, these truths can be difficult to adhere to. Take a look at these following simple truths and think of them as they pertain to marriage. They are true in most aspects of life but when they are applied to marriage, they become almost an entirely different set of guidelines to live by.

1. Treat those you love the most with the most respect and honor, even when they are wrong!
2. Love is your gift, not a wage someone earns. Making those you love earn your love creates within them resentment toward you.
3. All words have an impact. None can be taken back! Speak with love, respect, and thoughtfulness.
4. In marriage specifically, but in all relationships, be kind; be gentle; be thoughtful; be honest; be patient; by joyful; be faithful; be self-controlled.
5. Forgive; when you hold onto a wrong suffered it only keeps you suffering.

Relational Reality

6. Do good to those who treat you badly.
7. Treat all others the way you would like to treat.
8. Keep or develop a kind and fun sense of humor.
9. Never take yourself too seriously.
10. Be humble; never forget you are the creature, not the Creator!

In every relationship, these simple truths will take you far in life. The more you practice them, the more graceful your life and relationships will become.

Chapter 8

Love's evidence is creation. Personal creativity is our obvious reflection of the Creator. When we take that which we did not create or earn we diminish ourselves, we reject the nature of the Creator and refuse to honor and recognize his reflection in others. We deny reality.

YOU ARE CREATED IN the Creator's image. Physically? I do not know, maybe. We are definitely created in his creative nature. We too have creative natures, just like our Creator. We know the primary evidence of love is creation. Love is relational in all things for it is the very expression of the Creator. If we invest ourselves into family, friends, and work without the objective truth of the Creator as the genuine source, then our relationships become adrift in the subjective whims of all concerned. There is genuine emotional damage done when I am perceived as just a "player" in the subjective fiction rotating around someone for whom I care. It damages my self-esteem which filters down to all my relationships. Learning to be our true self is the Creator's plan for us all—the person he desires you to be. When we discover our true nature and direction for our lives we become self-actualized. There are many needs we all have. Let's look at what Maslow said about it.

No matter your age, social statu,s or religious preference, we all have a certain set of needs. There is a study tool known as

Relational Reality

Maslow's hierarchy which breaks down these very basic human needs. Maslow's approached posits that the most basic level of needs must be met before an individual will strongly desire the secondary or higher level needs.

This theory goes on to break down the basic human needs into subcategories to make it a little easier to digest. According to Maslow, human needs can be dissected as follows:

1. Physiological needs: air, w, food, sleep, clothing, shelter, sexual instinct
2. Safety needs: personal security, health, and well-being, financial security
3. Social needs: intimacy, belonging, family, and friendships

If you look closely at those categories, they share a few things in common, things that just about anyone can identify with. At the heart of everything listed in all three categories is the need to survive and then thrive: survive then thrive physically, survive then thrive intellectually, survive and then thrive emotionally. In each area, there is an objective reality which must be addressed. To weave a subjective fiction avoiding reality will only result in disaster. The connection to our Creator's world requires us to live in reality to our environment.

From an early point in our childhood, all humans start to feel a need to be wanted, desired, or respected in some way. While kids don't have the words for these things, it all boils down to the building up of self-esteem and self-respect. As the realization of the Creator's love and acceptance is personally intended for them, it builds a feeling of self-esteem, it provides them with encouragement to thrive and excel, to live in a way that leads to acceptance and value by others. As they grow older, these children will become adults that will choose careers that help to establish and feed this basic need for self-esteem. As they begin to reflect their creative purpose their true self-emerges: the person the Creator wants them to emerge as.

Chapter 8

On the other hand, people that grow up without a connection to objective relational reality are dependent upon the subjective fiction of others. Depending upon their role in that subjective fiction will determine just how little self-esteem they will have. They will often crave or feel a need for respect from others whom they view as an authority. They may become risk-takers who feel the need to seek fame or glory by placing their lives at risk in trivial ways. However, fame or glory will not help the person to build their self-esteem until they accept who they are internal. Psychological imbalances such as depression can hinder the person from obtaining a higher level of self-esteem. It makes it much harder to let go of our subjectivity and surrender to our Creator's objective purpose.

All people have a need for stable self-respect and self-esteem. There are two versions of esteem needs: an emotional version and an intellectual version. The emotional version of esteem caters to the need for respect from others. This may include a need for status, recognition, fame, prestige, or attention. But when we establish a subjective fiction around our lives this need becomes a burden which requires constant maintenance. When connected to the Creator and reality we are established emotionally and our self-esteem is reflective of the objective truth that we are held in high esteem as the very reflection of the Creator and are the recepient of his highest love. The intellectual version manifests itself as the need for self-respect. Standing in the knowledge we are created for a unique purpose as the one and the only person on the planet who can accomplish the Creator's intended specific purpose for each of us. With this confidence, a person is built upon a personal expression of strength, competence, mastery of the desired skill, and/or independence and freedom. This intellectual version enhances the emotional version because it relies on inner confidence established through personal experience with the Creator. Deprivation of these needs will lead to an inferiority complex, weakness, and helplessness. In other words, a life condemned to live in a self-centered subjective fiction.

To go somewhat deeper into this, we need to also look at another topic that is extremely important, and that is self-actualization. This is the desire to accomplish everything one can, to become the most that one can be. Individuals may perceive or focus on this need very specifically yet in very different ways. For example, one individual may have a strong desire to become an ideal parent while another has their dreams and goals set on becoming a master athlete. For some others, self-actualization might be expressed in paintings, pictures, sculptures, new inventions, and so on. As we are in the objective reality of our Creator's plan we have the freedom, the mandate to express ourselves creatively. We invest ourselves in those things that need to be done, then the things we enjoy and are passionate about.

Really, this self-actualization is the Creator's unique reflection in us as the individuals he created us to be and is the reason why all other needs exist. The meeting of all of our other needs to fully become the person we were meant to be is, in and of itself, the act of self-actualization. Without self-actualization, all other requirements are not truly met at all. There is only meaning for the fulfillment of all other needs when a person is able to self-actualize.

Again, this all starts to sound quite deep and complex. But one last word on the matter will, I think, help to summarize it into something we can all easily understand. The essence of self-actualization is creativity, and therefore creativity is the most basic of all human needs.

We all need to express ourselves. Self-actualization more or less proves this. We have the need to create how we experience our world (reality), ourselves (our place in reality), and our dreams (how we desire to create a reflection of who we are in fact). The need to experience safety, love, esteem, and well-being is to experience our true nature of dependence upon and reflection as creatures of the Creator. As reflections of the Creator, we also have the innate need to create.

Creativity is the ability to create something based on an idea—a self-generated thought or concept to change, adapt something, or a design to develop a wholly spontaneous new thing—art,

Chapter 8

music, stories, food, and on and on. It is the very expression of who the individual is as a combination of genetics, environment, and the unique spirit each person possess. And because of self-actualization, we also have a deep-rooted fear of criticism towards whatever it is that we created.

At our cores, we are each drawn to different things. We all have different likes, dislikes, passions, and fears. And that's what makes each persons' individual creativity unique. Think about when you were a child. Think of some of those make-believe games or scenarios you would envision while playing. When you were a child using your imagination to play bubbled up spontaneously. The same creativity that helped you to explore the world and learn new things as a child is still dwelling within you, and it is vitally important that we all remember that.

Every person is unique. Just as no two people have the same fingerprints, no two people have the same personal expressions of the Creator's nature. You and you alone have the ability to create a genuine reflection of that nature—of reality and purpose. Just as a violin player in an orchestra has a specific individual part to play, you too have an extraordinary role to play. But to play it, like that violin, you must be in tune—in tune with the objective reality of the Creator's love for you.

We've always dwelled on questions such as: "Who am I, really? Why am I here?" The answer lies within our own creativity. And we can start to answer that question for ourselves by starting with our Creator. We are, after all, his reflection. Our unique combination of intelligence, humor, likes and dislikes, appearance and body type, as well as culture and location, all combine together to show how creative he is.

We as humans are at our best when we discover that "calling." This usually presents itself as a career or hobby that we genuinely love—something that seems to fill us with purpose and meaning. It truly can be almost anything. We sink our hearts and soul as we enjoy the endeavors of our time and attention. The work of our hands and minds brings delight to the soul. We are at our best when we are reflecting the Creator and purpose in our lives.

Over the years, I have met many people who have fantastic ideas for new inventions or innovations to existing products. Nearly every single one of these people never followed through, though. And in the end, it has very little to do with the idea. More often than not, it was because they were never encouraged to be creatively adventurous. We all have these creative sparks, but we let the obstacles of our created subjective fictions get in our way. This robs us of a way of life that allows us to fully explore the objective truth of creation. As a reflection of the Creator, we should and can allow ourselves to create. Doing so will have a truly profound impact on you.

More than that, creativity can also be found and expressed through several of the nine factors we already discussed—more evidence of the Creator's encouragement for us to also be creators.

Love: Love what it is that you do and express it in what you create.

Joy: Whatever it is that you are creating should bring you and those that experience it joy.

Peace: Anything you create, when done correctly and for the right reasons and motivations, should bring you a degree of peace while creating it.

Patience: Remember those people I mentioned that I had met that had a great idea but ultimately abandoned it? A lack of patience can be just as harmful as a lack of encouragement. We must be patient with what we create if we want to give to the full attention it is due.

Kindness: Similar to joy and peace, anything you create should be offered to the world with a lens of compassion rather than confrontation or strife.

Self-control: If you plan to finish your creation successfully, it will take great restraint—not only to see it through to completion but to stick with it when things get tough or seem impossible.

As we intentionally reflect the Creator's nature we are adding more than just his goodness to the world—we are serving as his

Chapter 8

reflection. In all things, especially our creative endeavors, we are reflecting the Creator's goodness, kindness, and creativity to the world. Therefore, as we follow in his direction with our own creativity, we must present honest reflections of our hearts and our souls in obedience and reverence to him.

Chapter 9

Discovering the truth of the Creator establishes an objective platform. Developing subjective fictional accounts of reality and spreading them as if they were the objective truth is the verbal attempt to control others by bringing them into your subjective fiction.

So what can we take away from these accounts of subjective realities and objective truth? Yes, we all know the difference between fact and fiction, truth and lies. We are taught from childhood that it is a bad thing to lie—to fib or stretch the truth. But here and there, as we grow, we find ourselves telling little white lies. Some may seem harmless, like claiming you did, in fact, eat the broccoli your mother served you for dinner even though you managed to pocket it and then throw it in the trash can.

White lies eventually become bigger lies though. And before long, we don't even feel the slightest bit of regret from bending the truth or telling outright lies. And this can become a dangerous and treacherous slope.

You see, establishing a subjective falsehood as an objective reality will eventually force itself upon those you spend time with. It will entrap others into fiction that, if it remains unchecked, will erode your relationships. It places the one speaking falsehoods in the place of the Creator, bending the truth of reality to fit some

Chapter 9

other agenda or fabricated truth that fits better with your own wants and needs.

This is what happens when we make a habit of lying. There is really no end to a lie, as it goes on forever, always a part of your false reality. It does not honor truth, it does not respect the one to whom the lie is spoken to, and it certainly does not honor the Creator. It is merely a way to weave a subjective fiction for the enhancement of the speaker, usually to better their situation.

However, living in relational reality demands the honor of objective truth. This begins with understanding that there is an objective standard that was created by the Creator himself. Each person has that actual understanding built into their nature as part of his reflection (a reflection that we have already discussed as being visible to the world as we are a reflection of the Creator ourselves).

Truth is the objective reality of what, how, when, where, and who actually takes place regardless of any observation. When we experience objective truth, we filter it through our subjective lens and translate it using our genetic and environmental nature. That is why when two people see the same event or item, their descriptions can be radically different. Unless we are tethered to objective truth, we have no choice but to drift in and out of an objective reality.

Discovering the objective truth through our individuality and then working to express it through our creative endeavors is our purpose in life. We are created in the very image of the Creator, his nature expressed in us. But this nature can only be visibly and successfully expressed when we yield to his objective reality rather than the subjective fictions that have been created as a result of our self-centered understanding of the world around us. Without an understood and established a connection to his objective reality, we are doomed to wander in a subjective fiction we create for ourselves.

We begin to weave that fiction from the core of our being and then spread it through our subjective lens to others to bring them into our lives. Sadly, we often do this without even realizing that we are doing it, though we do sometimes shade the objective truth knowingly. But again, because we are accustomed to those small white lies from a young age, we sometimes don't feel remorse for it. Eventually, we begin to shade reality for falsehood intentionally. And the lie is born.

But when we are anchored in his relational reality—to his objective truth—our individual creativity is released in a unique and personal pattern with our surroundings. We become the true self we were created to be. Our true nature is revealed as we surrender our subjective fictions for his objective truth. This is a surrender that can best be played out through the creative directions he has implemented and will continue to embed in each one of us.

As we follow our passions under the Creator's objective guidance, we become our better selves. And while the word "surrender" might sound a bit harsh and make some want to cringe or hold on to that last stubborn bit of fiction, it is quite easy. This surrender is not something we have actually to do. Instead, it is merely who we are.

Each of us is a unique reflection of the Creator. As we yield to this truth, parts of us are slowly uncovered while others flourish and develop. It's much like the blooming of a flower as it opens itself to the sunlight. Yet because we are not rooted in the dirt and can move about, we have the distinct pleasure and advantage of having a choice: growing in the sunlight of relational reality or hiding in the lazy path by dwelling in the shadows of our own subjective fiction.

Establishing a subjective falsehood as objective reality necessarily seeks to entrap others in a fiction which necessarily by its very nature erodes relationships. It places the one speaking falsehood in the place of the Creator, trying to draw in another to their fictional portrayal of reality and setting them on a false course of understanding the objective truth. It does not honor fact; it does not respect the one to whom the lie is spoken to. It is merely a way to weave a subjective fiction for the enhancement of the speaker. Living in relational reality demands the honor of objective truth, beginning with the understanding that there is an objective standard created by the Creator himself. Each person has that objective understanding built into their nature as his reflection.

Truth is the objective reality of what, how, when, where, and who actually takes place regardless of any observation. When we experience objective truth, we filter it through our subjective lens and translate it given our genetic and environmental nature. That is why when two people see the same event, their description can be radically different. Unless we are tethered to the objective truth, we have no choice but to drift in and out of objective reality.

Discovering the objective truth through our individuality and expressing it in our creative passion is our purpose in life. We are created in the very image of the Creator, his nature expressed in us, but only as we yield to his objective reality, not a subjective fiction born of our self-centered understanding of the world around us. Without an understood and established a connection to his objective reality we are doomed to wander in a subjective fiction we create for ourselves.

When we begin to weave that fiction from the core of our being and then spread it through our subjective lens to others we bring them into our life story as bit players to our main character. We shade the objective truth knowingly or unawares to fit the fiction we have created for our lives. Eventually, we begin to intentionally cloud the reality for falsehood. The lie is born.

But when we are anchored in his relational reality (objective truth) our personal creativity is released in a unique and personal pattern in relation to our surroundings. We become the self we were created to be. Our true nature is revealed as we surrender our subjective fictions for his objective truth through the creative directions he has and will continue to embed in each of us.

As we follow our passions under the Creator's objective guidance through our yieldedness to his clear guidance in relational reality, we become our better selves.

This is not a something we have to do; quite frankly it is who we are. Each of us is a unique reflection of the Creator. Each of us as we yield to this truth is being uncovered even as a flower opens in the sunlight. But since we are not rooted in the dirt and can move about, ours is a choice to either flourish in the dynamic challenge in the sunshine of relational reality or to hide in the lazy path by dwelling in the shadows of our own subjective fiction.

Even when we are asked a hard question and answering it as truthfully as we could would hurt the questioner's feelings, living in relational reality demands honesty but not cruelty. We can respond with creative honesty while not explicitly answering the exact question. Being thoughtful in objective truth and wise in relationships requires maturity and practice within safe relationships.

Chapter 10

Being absorbed by another's creative results diminishes our own unique creativity and reflection of the Creator's specific objective for your life.

LIVING IN TODAY'S WORLD where one new gadget after another is being released, this is quite hard to do. Sometimes we can't help but be envious of that brand new phone or tablet, or really jealous of our neighbor's new car or our friend's new home. No matter how you paint it, this is coveting. And coveting does nothing more than make you feel inferior.

All you have to do to keep your heart from desiring what others have is to remind yourself of this elementary truth: You are the best person in the world in at least one personalized area! That is a guarantee!

Seriously. As generic and cheesy as it might sound, you are the best in the world at being you. You are the only one that can fit the mold the Creator has made for you. There is no one else out there exactly like you. You are a genuine creative individual with a truly unique perspective, enhanced with the nuance of your sole genetic and environmental combination brought together to reflect objective reality and your impact upon all within our relational sphere.

What this means is that no matter where you go—another country, the moon, Mars, some other galaxy—you are living proof of the Creator's love and desire for his creations. The Creator has placed you uniquely where you are in time and within relationships because he knew the fantastic creative potential you have. And he also was able to anticipate the vast need for it within the world.

It is tempting to covert the work of someone else. We all do it, often without knowing it. Think of a writer, just having finished their first book. They think it's a great book, but no one wants to publish it. Of course, this writer is going to look at best-selling authors and wish they had that same sort of success. By comparing their work to those that have mastered their craft, this new writer is automatically at a disadvantage. It is easy for the writer to judge his own work as inferior when compared to authors that are selling hundreds of thousands of copies.

Nonetheless, our best work is always a reflection of the Creator in us. As we grow in our craft, jobs, or passions, we start to realize that the actual relationship with the Creator is vested in the love of our own work. Going back to the writer above, if he is genuinely expressing himself in a way that is authentic and of the Creator, then he is genuinely rooted in and working out of the real objective reflection of the Creator's purpose for him. So coveting the achievements of others is unnecessary and degrading to not only himself but the Creator as well.

Dwelling on another's circumstances to the point of coveting or envy also creates a subjective fiction in our minds, which leads to bartering for other than the Creator's objective relational reality. This leads to relational damage in personal relationships, mainly if those we are covering are close to us.

Understanding this can be difficult, especially when we finally see the fiction we have woven around our lives. Breaking out of those habits and hang-ups is tough. To overcome this, we need to recognize that the Creator has placed us here for a reason—in our lives, in our environments, in our social and physical circles. He wants us to excel where we are, using creativity to express who we are as individuals. He does not wish a copy-and-paste group of people, but unique individuals that can uniquely reflect him in countless different ways.

At any given point in time, in our unique circumstances, regardless of how we got there, the Creator wants us to live in a relational reality. He wants us centered in objective relational reality to him while we establish the actual fact of truth, genuine relationships with others, and our environment.

Absorbing these truths of objective reality will shock us back into a pattern of dynamic life. Think about it . . . each morning we wake up with a new creative potential to be productive in our own unique place with family, friends, and within our work. And we get to do it not only to further ourselves and express our creativity but to make much of the Creator.

Also, did you notice the mention of work above? That's an important one to remember. The Creator has plans for you at work too. You need to express your creativity and individual reflection of him there also. Even at work, we must remember that we have the potential to impact people everywhere (including work) and to present them with our reality rather than an extension of the fictions that the world casually presents them with.

So when we are able to be an authentic reflection of the Creator everywhere, under any circumstances, we start to get a much better grip on relational and objective reality. The key, however, is to realize that wanting the success someone else has achieved or that expensive car or house is an ingrained fiction that the world pushes on us. Only after we have accepted that we are wonderfully made as a unique individual for a reason known only by the Creator can we genuinely reflect him in the workplace, in our homes and neighborhoods, and the world at large.

Applying these profound truths in our daily lives and relationships is a challenge. Living in such a way requires more grace and righteousness that we have. Each of us falls short at one time or another. We all miss the mark. We all have known the lie and the truth and chosen to tell the lie. We have all at one time or another known the right thing to do and picked the wrong.

The Creator himself stepped into time and placed upon himself the results of our shortcomings. Jesus, the very Son of God, took the penalty. He set his body between us and the ultimate outcome of our personal sin. Personally and individually accepting his sacrifice for us and allowing his Holy Spirit to rebuild and teach us through our faith in him enables us to build a life of relational reality starting with the Creator himself. The plan is simple yet often hard to do.

Chapter 11

*Empowerment for living in relational reality
is the Creator's plan.*

BEING EMPOWERED BY THE Creator's life makes all the difference in the world. It transcends dependence upon others to our reliance upon he who knows us best and loves us the most. It is his Spirit living within us which enables us to live a life genuinely reflective of his purpose in creating us as the Joy of his realized love. We are unique individual reflections of his reality.

Living in his relational truth frees us from being dependent or reactionary to those with who we are in a relationship. How they speak, act, or behavior as we live in relational reality no longer determines how we respond. We can talk now in love and kindness to hateful attacks. This is what Jesus was talking about when he said to turn the other cheek. We can now take the hurt and bitterness which is in the world and, rather than reacting to it, we can proactively speak loving, healing truth to the hurting hearts.

Living in relational reality frees us from the circumstances of life and allows us to act instead of reacting to the challenges of life. We no longer need fear the outcome of any given event for his will for us is to live a proactive life. Regardless of what happens for good or bad we now can relate to any incident with clarity of heart and mind as we live in our created purpose. It is his actual Spirit residing within us draws us to him. But we do have a choice. What will you choose?

Will you choose a life guided by subjectivity? Are you living a life which has been created and is governed by your personally created fiction about life? Are you living a life choosing to ignore the objective truths of reality, hoping against hope everything will just work out in the end if you just do your own thing, live in your own "reality"?

You are singularly unique. The Creator has placed in you his stamp of approval. But for it to become "activated" into that perfect place of relational reality with our Creator so he can mold you into that perfect you which he has in mind, you have to accept his gift with honesty about who you are what all you have done living in your subjection fictions, and with humble gratitude.

Accept the gift of his Son's sacrifice for you. For the cross of Christ is the very center of objective relational reality.

He left the church as a group of friends and family built around a new relationship with Christ at the center. The old pattern of organized religious ritual has been replaced with a band of supernatural relationships, people with no other than to live in objective truth encouraging one another to live as the unique reflections of the Creator empowered by Jesus' Holy Spirit in each of us.

The only reason that Jesus came to earth was to make wrong relationships right, first by reconciling us to the Creator, then by reconciling our relationships with one another.

God's love moved Moses to write the Ten Commandments, or the fundamental principles for healthy relationships. Jesus fulfills the mandate for living in relational reality and then enables us to walk the same path. His graceful Spirit of love empowers us to love each other even as he has loved us. He gave us each other to practice these ten principals and encourage us each to reflect the Creator as only we can.

But sin erodes who we are as well as those we love the most. Sin is an acid that eats away at the most lovable parts of our being and then even seeps into nature. Sin is what enables me to choose

Chapter 11

myself instead of putting those I love first. As a believer, I ask how, why? Where is God when temptation comes with a force that is irresistible? Where is the church and support system that is to build a "firewall" and prevent, heal, protect, and help develop strength where these relationships are weak and vulnerable before they come to destruction?

Where is the reality? Where is the honesty? Where is the integrity? There is none! Not in the areas where we are weakest. That is why Jesus died for us, because there is a part of ourselves that we cannot control! Our sin nature is beyond our control as individuals! In a growing number of cases in the church, it is adultery. But in thousands, perhaps millions of others in the church the uncontrollable sin is an acceptable sin to be a gossip or a liar or a backbiter, cheat at taxes or in business, or any number of private "faults" that we have learned to put up with. These sins Jesus said were as bad as any.

Many Christians will say if you just trust in the Holy Spirit and the Bible God says that he will give you the words to say when you need them and that he will not put on you more than you can bear. It is true, yet the many who love God more than their own lives fall, just as you and I do on a regular basis. Many of these are great (public) sins that bring shame to Jesus and his body and are evidence of a great need in the body of Christ in America. That need is not for more information (Bible study), or more structure; it is a need for healthy, transparent people living in relational reality!

For years in America this pattern of public sin, due to closed-off hearts, has repeated itself daily in the lives of pastors and leaders in the church as well as with the laity. The reputation of Christ has fallen on hard times because of the continuing immoral behavior of his followers. Yet all of his followers are immoral. No doubt about that!

Where is the moral fiber to stand? Where is the inner healing of the heart when it comes to behavior? (Now don't look to any man, for if you do you will only see one who acts like there is no secret sin that he struggles with.) The building blocks of healthy emotional adults and teenagers have been lost, and the failure of the church leaders to stem the tide in their own families is a testimony to the collapse of the way that the church in America is functioning.

The confession of sin, a genuinely repentant heart, and a willingness to allow the church to restore broken fellowship seem to ring hollow even when all that we know to do has been done. Yet still the system fails (not all the time, just about 80 percent of the time)!

The power of the Spirit of God seems to be missing in the church of the living God. The church in America has a form of godliness, yet it has no power to even halt the streaming destruction of sin in its own families. Thus, as is evident to all that care to look, the moral behavior of those within the church is no different than the surrounding community who are not part of the church. This is the very pattern of church life that is followed in America and is being exported by its mission agencies.

Never before on the planet has the "gospel" been preached so clearly as it is being preached in America today. Any time of day or night anywhere in America anyone can listen to and or watch Christians explaining the good news about Jesus. Yet moral behavior in America continues to move away from biblical teachings. The churches continue to decline, and America is a "post-Christian" nation. How can this be when the Word is being preached every minute of every day on every square inch of the United States?

The answer is as simple as seeing what is wrong with playing football on a baseball field. Christians have been so deceived by the enemy that most do not even know what the field of battle is.

The organized church in America, for the most part, is relationally dysfunctional (there are exceptions). Across denominational lines, regardless of the theology or view about miracles, the Christian church—liberal or conservative, charismatic or evangelical, independent or denominational—holds to a system that seems to be powerless to have a permanent effectual change in behavior. Not just in their neighborhoods and communities but also in the lives of their own parishioners.

Chapter 11

God will bless whatever we let him. Many are coming to know him through this weak system because of his grace and truth, yet most will either drop out or become so complacent that it would be better if they were just dead cold. The 80/20 rule rules every organized church in America; no more than 20 percent of Christians in America's churches assume any responsibility. None involved in church leadership can deny with integrity the truth of what is written here! The current secret to an "organized" church growth is to have a bigger front door than the back door. Even the "lay" leadership of churches has a limited lifespan of effectual service before they burn out or drop out or turn off and just go through the now meaningless motions.

There is a better way! The pattern of natural church life is bright and open to being lived by all willing to trust God in reality, rather than in hollow, albeit well-meaning speech.

The pattern of life has been opened to us by Jesus. This is the pattern of church relational reality: believers anchored to learning how to live within these ten principles, reflecting his creative grace uniquely as his chosen individuals banded together to reflect love acceptance and forgiveness, so woven together it is grace personified. Jesus came to fulfill these principles in the lives of his people.

In Jesus the "Law" is complete! It is enabled, not removed. No longer legalistic laws, they have become the very principals for life with which we believers have been empowered!

Living in the ten principles for relational reality has been established for us as the pattern for who we are in Christ! It is the "new wine skins" for believers!

Living in relational reality provides the way today to have an overwhelming joy and spiritual strength that rivals the New Testament. This is the way which is supernatural to the surrounding secular world but very natural in Christian lifestyles.

Balance in life is founded in right relationships. First, an inner balance that can only come from the Creator, and then the outward balance that just comes from a proper relationship with others.

Relational Reality

The only reason that Jesus came to earth was to make wrong relationships right, first by reconciling us to the Creator and then to spread this good news by reconciling our relationships with one another. The good news is that God loves me. His love brings genuine, meaningful healing and if I allow him, he will enable me to love those around me the same way he loves me.

His body is to extend that reconciliation of relationships, not as a byproduct of religious education or a hoped-for product of "ministry," but as a natural part of who they are: Jesus' body on the earth.

Christians have been purchased by the blood of Jesus, to reflect his life in them. Not to try and live a better life! His life is one of love, acceptance, and forgiveness. Not one of organized mindless ritual. There is a way to do this, there is a pattern of church life that is meaningfully joyful to live and incredibly uplifting to be involved with: an experience that reflects him, not us!

The time has come to stop living an unnatural kind of Christianity and begin to live the natural sort of Christlike life his Holy Spirit indwelling power imparts to his body.

The moment Jesus set foot on this earth his life became natural. It is time for us all to live in the relational reality of natural Christianity. Living as his reflections of his creativity uniquely expressed in each of us. His body we encourage to live in relational reality by sustaining each other to reflect the unique creation he has designed each of us to be. When we are anchored to his objective reality, we are free to be subjectively creative.

Chapter 12

Jesus came to make wrong relationships right.

THE OVERARCHING TRUTH OF Jesus' life is that he came to reconcile self-deceived man to righteous God and to provide a pattern for living in this fallen world. To accomplish this he spent thirty-three years on this earth.

Thirty of those years he had no public ministry that we know of and the best evidence says that he remained home with his family during those first thirty years.

During the next three years of "public" ministry, he spent somewhere between 75 to 90 percent of his time with twelve men. The pattern of life that the God-man lived was one of deep investment into his important relationships. That is the pattern that he expected his disciples to follow! Personal investment in relational reality!

Jesus said that he only did what he saw the Father do. He copied what God the Father did. The pattern of life that he lived by investing his life into a small group of people, then, is the pattern that exists within the Holy Trinity! Relational at its core! Coequal yet honoring one another before self, and in doing that very thing building oneself without intent.

It is my belief that God desires Jesus' body in the world today, his church, to reflect the very kind of life that Jesus manifested. A Jesus kind of life, which requires a social context of equality, love, and preference of others before self. One which is entirely and honestly built around transparent relationships above all things on the earth. Relationships which reflect the very nature of God: unconditional, unqualified love. Encouraging each other to live uniquely as God's very creative creations.

There is no more normal and natural way of living on the earth than the plan that was model by Jesus and his disciples. The fantastic part about God's love is his willingness to accept anyone without reservation.

Through observing and learning about the nature of God, the church, and the Bible, I believe that we can have a fuller mental understanding of this truth, but no one will really grasp the reality of "God in you the hope of glory" until they have surrendered in total to the living God. Once that complete surrender takes place his Holy Spirit through his body (the church) will genuinely transform that one into a new creature in Christ.

No longer do you have to live emotionally isolated or fearful. No longer do you have to solely trust the professional "clergy" to help you understand. No longer does anyone need a "shaman" to explain the "hidden mysteries" of deep spirituality. For the church's corporate and individual purpose is for no other reason other than to bring love, joy, peace, patience, goodness, gentleness, kindness, faithfulness, and self-control to you and those you love. This is fruit of Christian's life. We love as Jesus himself loves, reflecting his intention, God's very own nature: LOVE without qualification and without reservation.

Every person alive has a great void in their life. That void is the place that we so often try to fill with sex, drugs, work, marriage, children, etc., yet all of us know none of those things really fills the deep emptiness. There is a part of each person that only a proper relationship with their Creator can fill and produce an inner balance.

The door that this balance comes through is the gracious gift of life that Jesus provided for us. His death on the cross is the fulfillment of God's great love for us. For God took that most loved part of himself, his Son, and gave up that special relationship and

Chapter 12

allowed through Jesus' open wounds passage for you and me into the core of God's own life of love, which results in our proper relationships. That begins with inner healing of the natural fault line that lies within each of us.

Now there is a problem. It lies in these fault lines, or sin, or that part of us that allows us to lie when we know the truth, or to chose the wrong when we know the right thing to do, or to entertain those thoughts which we are so ashamed about.

That part of our nature which is faulty, the sin in us, must be honestly confronted. As in any good relationship, God expects us to be totally honest. He supplies the way and power; we provide the truth about ourselves. The concepts of confession and repentance of sin are an old way of saying I just tell God the truth about myself and those parts which God does not like, and I don't want in my life anymore. It is that simple and clear.

The pain and reality of life lie in the cost of breached relationships. Because of the sin in our lives, the only way that God could bring balance was for him to open his life to us.

Jesus' death on the cross brought justice and payment, or balance, and thereby provided an avenue for us to enjoy God's love and healthy relationship in our life and then to translate that loving kind of healthy relationship to those we love.

The priority of his life in our innermost being is necessary for us to have a healthy balance in order to love others from a "nonselfish" perspective. He births this new life in us, but unless there is a friendly environment in which this new life finds itself, it will shrink into a dark place in the hearts of people and the last state is worse than the first. They know the truth of God's love relationship, but they have not found the proper environment in which that which was birthed in them, can survive and even thrive! That environment had its foundation in God's very nature and was modeled by Jesus to his disciples and then passed on from his disciples to the churches.

God's nature and his expression of his nature to us through the environment in which he has given us to live in is evidence of his existence and his purpose for our lives.

Relational Reality

Relationships are messy! That is one of the things that scares me about God. He has a will that requires things of me. In the past his will has been "taught" in terms that place burdens on people that seem almost ridiculous: "Do good always (eat only with your right hand), don't do bad things ever (don't work on Sundays), go to church on Sundays, don't fart in public, and don't eat shellfish or pork, etc." What if this God, this all-powerful being, decides that he doesn't like me anymore? What then? When bad things happen to people, does that mean God is mad at them? Would a loving God really let so many people go through so much hurt in this world? These issues of life argue the point that the absence of pain and struggle are the ultimate good.

In God's plan of life, those things which force us to deal with the real issues of life and not just be caught up in the visible or superficial things have a high priority. He does not willingly allow his any of his creatures to go through needless pain, yet at the same time he will not exempt any from the struggles of life when those very struggles force us to deal with reality.

From the nature of our physical bodies, we know that pain is for our ultimate good. It is a bodily system to warn of us of danger. On a grander scale, the problems and pain of life are also part of the world's system to notify us of a greater threat. That danger is a lack of balance or breached relationships internally and externally.

Therefore, when a society begins to lose its internal balance of healthy relationships, things like crime and family dissolution, and excessive laws to try and control the problems spreading, become evident.

When the geography of an area loses its natural balance or proper relationship to the surrendering area, the resulting pain is inflicted upon those living that are causing the problem or can repair the problem. Of course, there is also a "self-repair" aspect to nature, that when what is out of balance is stressing the environment, it can and does repair itself, without regard to living beings.

Since the very nature of God (the part that we have been allowed to see) has its expression in a corporate sense—Father, Son, and Holy Spirit—the greatest good is in the balance of healthy relationships. Since even in creation that need for balance, proper relationship, drives nature itself, we can know that it is God's clear will for us to live a life that is defined by how we love and interact with him and others. The pain and suffering that accompanies life is the correcting process that forms and shapes us to stay focused in reality and not in the fault line that causes sin or those breaches in our inner lives that call us to a self-above-all mentality or in our behavior.

Human history is the history of how people relate to one another. Physical sciences are the study of how different aspects of the universe relate to one another. Sociology is the study of how cultures relate to one another. Every part of our lives has a relational context. But for those related contextual parts of our lives, we must have a center point or a proper relational balance internally. If we do not then the spin of our lives will spin out of control, like a tire out of balance, and sooner or later it will cause a breakdown.

There has never been a society (that we know of) that has not had a God or gods to guide them. It is a built-in kernel of human nature to want to be part of something larger than themselves. There is a pang of hunger inside of every human that points them to a search for God.

Again our very nature tells us that if there is a hunger built into us, there is a way to satisfy that hunger. God is made evident in the very relational aspect of the earth, the stars, and our own nature which has been created in the image of God!

Even as we are created in his image in a social context, we are internally created in his image. There are three aspects to our own individual natural: spirit, soul, and body. So even in an internal way we must be in a relational harmony within our being. When a tennis player wants to become better at tennis, she hires a coach. The most respected coaches are the "player-coaches" who can not only teach but also perform.

There is such a spiritual "player-coach": Jesus, the God-man, who even though he never traveled further than one hundred miles from his home, has all of time measured by his life.

Jesus is the "player-coach" for our lives, and by emerging from his presence we can become all that our Creator and we want us to be.

Spiritual truth is transcendent. It applies to every aspect of human life.

The truth of relational balance internally and externally is a law of life established as part of our very nature. To deny this truth is to pretend that we really don't need our eyes to see or our ears to hear. To deny the reality most of us at one time or another experience in our own lives is to block out a vital part of who we are and miss that part of life that brings the greatest joys.

Jesus had as his express purpose to make way for everyone to enter into harmony with God. He came to empower each of us to be the singularly unique reflection of the Creator. He came to provide that avenue. Even as a circle must be broken to allow entrance, Jesus opens the door for all. God in his completeness entered the earth in Jesus and gave us a model that was so profound that time is measured by his life. In other words, the very time we measure our lives by is understood relative to Jesus' life!

In the Bible, in John chapter 17, we have a unique opportunity to listen into a conversation with Jesus talking to God the Father (or God speaking to himself out loud for our benefit). Listen to what he says:

> Verse 3: "This is eternal life, that they may know You, the only true God, and Jesus Christ whom You have sent." (This is not intellectual knowledge, but a knowing like Adam knew Eve; this is a relational concept!)
>
> Verses 21–23: "that they may all be one; even as You, Father, {are} in Me and I in You, that they also may be in Us, so that the world may believe that You sent Me. The glory which You have given Me I have given to them, that they may be one, just as We are one; I in them and You in Me, that they may be perfected in unity, so that the world may know that You sent Me, and loved them, even as You have loved Me."

Chapter 12

Verse 26: "and I have made Your name known to them, and will make it known, so that the love with which You loved Me may be in them, and I in them."

The obvious concern that Jesus had was for the unity of his people! They are in a proper relationship with God and each other. In John chapter 13 Jesus clearly says that the way that people will know his followers is how they love one another! There is nothing in Scripture that speaks so clearly that the identifying mark of God in a person's life is how they love each other.

The whole of Jesus' life was one of reflecting the Father's love through his life by investing a deep intimate love in his followers. He then told them to go and make disciples. The only pattern of disciple-making that they had was the way that he had invested his life in them. The only pattern of life that Jesus reflected was that of the Godhead! That kind of life, then, is the genuine "natural" life that is God's plan for us, is and was from the beginning a reflection of his presence and love. A properly related group of peers loving one another is the expression or the living image of God on earth.

The focus of Jesus' life was to bring forgiveness of sin and reconciliation with God and others. His pattern of life was to be our pattern of life, and the rebuilding or proper relationships was/is the core of direction.

The terms that Jesus spoke in were misunderstood continuously by the religious of the day. He would talk in terms of relationships: love, grace, forgiveness, mercy, acceptance. But the religious would translate those healing concepts into work systems which had to be performed for one to be "right" with God.

His personal goal and purpose concerning old religious systems was one of completeness. He viewed himself as the ending of the religious systems used to reflect the shortcomings of people. All religious systems have a vested interest in keeping people "sinners" (or in need of the special information that the enlightened or clergy say they possess), therefore all need the services of the "righteous" (enlightened) to help them grow in their understanding of God. He was not saying that the things sincere religious people (even clergy) do are be bad or wrong; he merely said that in him was the completion of the final product. That those systems were no longer necessary because in his person and in his relationship to all creation proper life-giving relationships can and will be restored. The need for a religious work system was a pattern of life whose purpose was to demonstrate the great need mankind has for reconciliation that can only come from God. Jesus is that reconciliation to bring a healthy balance to our relationships, first with God than with others.

Jesus' demonstration is one of simple balanced relational living. This is offered as a free gift, that no one should charge for. Jesus clearly spoke to those he sent out, "Freely you have received, freely give." His followers clearly understood that they as his followers should never expect pay for that which by its very nature is free.

The religious leaders began to understand that he was speaking against the way they received their ego gratification and self-esteem (and to some degree even their livelihood). Jesus was clearly speaking against religious organizations being used for profit and any selfish level as well as to lift any person above another. When he spoke, Jesus continually focused on the difference between God's kind of life for people and the nature of religious life that religious organizations sell (market) to people. Again, this is the difference between grace and work. The religious of the day had a vested interest in people being dependent upon them, to help them "get right with God."

Jesus' focus was in bring healing at all levels in a person's life. He sought out those places and times where his character and the nature of his person would best be understood by his actions and behavior. The general pattern of his life was to live as an example so that the message was the man rather than the man having a message. His instruction was for his followers to model the life that he had modeled before them. The emphasis was always on the relationships that they had with each other and God.

When they asked him to teach them to pray, the focus was on the relationship: "Our Father." It begins with a relational position, rather than an authority/servant position. The lesson in prayer ends with relational teaching of how to react when a breach in a human relationship occurs.

It also had a reminder that our relationship position with the Father is reflected in our relationships with others. When they ask him the most important issues of life, his response was to remind them of the great commandment of God: "Love God and love your neighbor as yourself!" Again totally relational!

When asked to condemn sinners, his reply was to ask the accuser to identify with the sinner. "Who among you is without sin." When asking about the nature of his person, he only spoke regarding his relationship with the Father. When asking how he performed the miracles, he again answered in relational terms: "What I see the Father do I do, what I hear the Father say, that is what I say."

When he taught on leadership, it was so remarkably different in that he demonstrated the real kind of leadership that he expected in his followers. He began to wash their feet physically. The point being that leadership that follows Christ's example serves in a very literal way. In contrast, the organized religious leadership twisted the concepts of servanthood into a rare art form of doublespeak; i.e., the servant-leader! "I get to be in front, and I get to be paid, and I get to have special privilege. I am gifted to serve by being in the front, on the top and receiving special treatment. I am the clergy."

Their interest was more than just monetary; it also was ego investment. They perceived themselves as a "specially gifted and called" group set aside by God for a higher purpose. They were the clergy, the priest.

The healings he performed brought balance back to twisted, sick spirits, souls, and bodies. He even addressed some sickness as sin! The clergy of the day saw the healings through a context that placed more value on the system than it did the person. Thus they defined healings through a system of organized behavior and teachings, with the clergy well in control. He meant that this person had missed the mark of balance with nature and God and others. The result was broken, out-of-balance people. They meant that the solution to the problem of people would come through yielding their lives to the teaching and instruction of Scripture as interrupted by the clergy. Again it was a control issue. Jesus allowed those he healed and those he was about to heal complete freedom, while the clergy required strict control of action.

As twenty-first-century believers we are dependent upon two very real aspects of God: the fellowship of believers in honest relationship uniquely reflecting Jesus to each other and the world. We are also dependent upon the reality of the Holy Spirit in each of us as comforter and teacher: God the Creator's very presence within every Christian.

Chapter 13

Spiritual reality

THERE IS NOTHING IN science, physics, or biology which can explain how lifeless material (particles) became self-aware or conscious. There is an "otherness" to life which is a mystery, unexplained and mostly ignored by science. The reality is we exist separate or above or beyond our simple physical bodies. We, our soul or spirit or consciousness, are not simply an algorithm which if reproduced properly will result in self-awareness. There is a reality to our otherness from all other creation.

The first clue: We live (have an awareness outside the material world) beyond our physical existence. After extensive research, an acceptable common understanding of spirituality has never been recognized by the major religions or scientists of the world ... ever.

To say there is a common understanding is a stretch. Each from its emotional core builds a different universe or worldview and brings with it a divergent concept of spirituality. Many people think in terms of emotions; the way they feel dictates how they think. The circumstances of their lives create a bubble around their thinking. Emotions are the connections in our minds to our physical feelings. They can be influenced by physical pain, a headache, a hangnail, a sore knee, or even the weather. Therefore how we feel may not the best way to determine how we think.

But if we go back to the basic definition of the word "spirit," the vast majority of languages define "spirit" as breath, wind, air, blow, breathe . . . not a big help! But it is a definite clue! To quote Holmes: "Now the game is afoot!"

Think about it as those who lived thousands of years ago did. Across cultures, languages, geography, and time past the best way to capture an understanding of a reality we all experience but cannot identify is the idea of air and wind. It moves things, brings refreshment, brings enjoyment and pleasure, brings warnings of what is about to come, disturbs the environment (air) we breathe and need to exist. When deprived of it, we faint or die. We cannot see, taste, touch, or knowingly experience its reality unless it is bringing or involved with something other than itself.

In applying this analogy to understanding the "spirit" in our human experience, we will need to approach it from a balanced perspective. Take the ancient and current cross-cultural understandings, blend them with personal knowledge, then mix this with a goodly portion of sacred writings. What we get is an actual understanding of authentic spirituality.

So the starting point is an understanding that every culture which has ever existed has recognized the existence of the "spirit" and in trying to define it and understand it requires an acceptance that things exist beyond our understanding, beyond of experience, something out there which we live in, in fact, need it to survive but when we tried to deal with it directly is allusive. It is common in human experience to receive hints and brief encounters with that which is "other."

Sticking with the analogy, when our encounter with this kind of thing is profound (like a hundred-mile-an-hour wind), if we survive, we don't forget and it changes us emotionally and/or intellectually. Now move this to someone you know or have heard about who has had a profound encounter with the "spiritual." Sound the same?

So the folks (the ancients, transcultural) who brought us language, different philosophies, together with the building blocks for

Chapter 13

rational, thought laid the foundation for understanding the reality of spirituality.

To speak about it they used the best way to explain its existence; the analogy of wind or air is like authentic spirituality. It exists; we can't see it, but we can experience it. It provides a life for us while bringing us refreshment (like a cool breeze on a hot day), enjoyment (the sound of music in the air), pleasure (fragrance of honeysuckle in the wind), and restoration (when we are out of breath). It can bring us warnings—the smell of rain in the air or worse. If you have ever been near a tornado, you know how the air and wind change to a genuine presence of warning. And if we don't heed the warning, then it brings disaster and destruction!

So living in actual spirituality, we can determine it is like living in the wind or air. We recognize and are thankful for its existence. We pay attention to its influence upon us as we live our daily lives. It is one of the environments in which we live. It does not matter if we acknowledge it or not; we need it to survive; lose it and we die; enhance it, protect it, and our lives become better.

It is true some folks are more aware of their surroundings than we are (weathermen, for example . . . just joking). The older we get and have more life experience, the more aware of the air around us, the more sensitive we become to what the wind is bringing.

I broke my leg as a teenager. The doctor told me it would be just fine till I was older. Then he said I would be able to tell when the weather was changing by the pain in my leg. I am sixty-eight now. He was totally correct! The weather (now we know barometric pressure) influences my internal bone structure which has mended yet is more vulnerable to atmospheric pressure than usual.

There is an unseen influence in our lives beyond the physical which reflects and shapes reality. Our consciousness or self-awareness reveals itself in our wonder and searches for meaning. There is an old argument: For every basic need we have as humans there is satisfaction. We need to breathe, and there is air; we need to drink, and there is water; we need to eat, and there is food; and we need to love, and there are others to invest ourselves in; we hunger for answers, and therein lies another clue . . .

Actual spirituality is an innate awareness of that part of ourselves and life around us which transcends just physical experience. It is that part of which makes us hunger for ultimate truth and answers.

Keeping the analogy alive, not as a literary tool for changing a mind but as the primary way spirituality has been spoken of and understood transculturally throughout the ages, the very best way to understand the reality of spirituality is by speaking of it as wind or the very air we breathe.

We don't have to be aware of the air to experience it. It is there whether we believe it or not. We see the effect of it or the impact of a lack of it. When we do realize it exists it can become a tool for us: blowing up balloons, creating a fan to cool, understanding aerodynamics thus flight.

We also know that we possess air inside our bodies and we can blow our breath and create a brief wind. Even so, spirituality is both outside us and inside us, objective and subjective. So to talk about the intangible aspect of human life and experience those who created our languages used the word "spirit," therefore we are in fact at least partially spiritual beings.

When the spirit leaves the body, we die. In fact, a primary way to know if the life has left a person is if they are breathing or air has been cut off for several minutes. To revive a person one of the more common methods is to breathe our air into them.

We all experience the reality of spirituality, just as we all experienced air. Most just ignore it until there is a problem with it, then we realize something dire in our life is amiss.

We realize the reality of spirituality. The experience becomes a curiosity, then becomes a thought process which takes us into an investigation.

Many at this point get distracted by the things associated with or being delivered by the spirit itself, just as it is easy to be distracted by the air when it is filled with smoke. It is amazing how many folks think those who talk about spiritual things are "just

Chapter 13

blowing smoke" when the smoke is an emotional predisposition to avoid anything they perceive as threatening, uncomfortable, strange, or different.

So spirituality is the realization of the existence of an essential part of life. It is not readily visible, but necessary to live; it is a part of life which has an impact upon our health and well-being. It at the same time can bring attention to our lives and our environment even before we fully know or see the issue being brought to us (like a pleasing fragrance or like smoke in the air as a warning of a fire). It almost subconsciously alerts us, it exists on the edge of our awareness, yet we are a washed in it.

The reality of a spiritual existence was understood by the folks who brought us language, a basic understanding of philosophy (or ways of thinking), and civilization. The language used illustrated the best context for understanding. Like it or not, there is a spiritual component to life.

Spirituality realized means merely an awareness of reality and openness to the experiences it already is bringing into who we are. We are all spiritual beings as well as physical beings.

There are touchstones in our lives which provide evidence to the reality of our spiritual existence. As we mature we begin to discover those touchstones.

The entrance to realization is our humble gratitude to the Creator. When we come to full realization that we are the creatures, not the Creator, regardless of our life circumstances, we can begin to appreciate the remarkable environment and world around us.

Some of these touchstones are love, creativity, wonder, imagination, profound relational connection, and original thought.

Even the laboratories of today's physicists are discovering on the subatomic level that mere human observation has an impact upon the physical. There is a reality to our spirituality. To deny this is to deny what it means to be human.

Chapter 14

Relational balance!

KNOWING NOW THAT SPIRITUALITY exists both inside and outside us kind of traps us in the middle. No worries, this is a good thing. It creates balance. Relationships are a balancing act, keeping ourselves centered while interacting with others around us while living and working in an environment which is disjointedly trying to knock us off center.

Thinking for ourselves again, setting aside our biases and once again venturing into open-mindedness, think of balance like a gyroscope or a wheel on a car.

In a healthy existence, all things have balance. From the astronomical to energy and material, to the environmental, the atomic, the chemical, to personal relationships, and in our emotions, there must be a balance for harmonious existence and understanding and even for life to exist.

In all things, there is and must be an internal balance (or weight: center of gravity) and an externally balanced relationship with all within its sphere of relations.

Balance establishes stability. It keeps things centered. It keeps things in an appropriate relationship to its core value. Every object, in reality, has internal centeredness of gravity; an inherent weight of existence, if you will.

Chapter 14

At the basic level: the hydrogen atom. Let me drift into more of a scientific model for just a moment: The motion of the electron circling the hydrogen atom occurs in three dimensions, and there is also a force acting on the electron (balancing, the internal weight, and the external centrifugal force).

This force, the electrostatic force of attraction, holds the atom together. The magnitude of this force is given by the product of the nuclear and electronic charges divided by the square of the distance between them.

The electron is confined to move on a line; the total energy is entirely kinetic in origin since no forces were acting on the electron (it is in balance).

In the hydrogen atom, however, the energy of the electron, because of the force exerted on it by the nucleus, will consist of potential energy (one which depends on the position of the electron relative to the nucleus) as well as kinetic energy.

What all this means is just that the hydrogen atom is the most stable element known. It is in almost perfect balance with an internal weight of existence and an external rotating electron creating an almost perfect balance on the surface of the atom. When one destroys or tries to split the stability of this atom, one gets a nuclear (or hydrogen) bomb! Not a good thing to mess with the balance of reality.

Let's look at the macro or vast scale: our solar system.

Our solar system is made up of the sun and everything that travels around it. Our eight planets and their natural satellites, such as Earth's moon; dwarf planets such as Pluto and Ceres, as well as asteroids, comets, and meteors. The sun is the center of our solar system. It contains almost all of the mass in our solar system and exerts a tremendous gravitational pull on planets and other bodies. The earth is the planet in a perfect relationship (distance, rotation rate, etc.) to the sun for enabling life to exist.

Again what this means is just that the sun is the center of our system and is by far the single most influential factor in our life-enhancing environment. Therefore do not mess with the balance of the solar system or life on Earth will cease to exist.

Relational Reality

From the smallest known element to our solar system, the universe in its totality has a fantastic balance. We live in a balance of internal and external realities of any given point of reference. It gives us a basic understanding of another aspect of our spiritual life which we cannot see, but experience. When things are out of balance at any level, we all know it.

The center point or internal weigh of reality is the Creator. You are one of those points of reference. You exist! You have balance! At birth, you are a solid point of reference, with the internal need for balance or centeredness (primarily physical: food, sleep being kept clean, etc.) and an external demand for relational balance and a need for balance in the ("awe" or wonder, the creative) spiritual realm. How a child becomes a healthy person as they grow depends upon the balance.

1. As a new person, you have physical awareness (or balance physically), so you do exist physically. Your body makes you physically aware of "otherness," that which exists physically which is not you.

2. As a new person, you have intellectual awareness (or the maturing thought process that establishes an understanding of self) so you do have a soul or independent self-existence separate of others.

3. As a new person, you have spiritual awareness (or the wonder of the unknown forced by physical birth connected with the spark of creation; the wonder, the need to express yourself in creative ways) so you do exist spiritually.

4. As a new person, you also have an emotional awareness. This is where your physical five senses (the physical input into your intellectual awareness) merge with your intellect while searching for spiritual validation. (Quite often this comes out as the "aught" or "that's not fair" principle, a call to that which is beyond desiring justice or "balance.")

The remainder of our lives is a dance of developing and then keeping balance, which sucks when your sense of balance is as bad as

Chapter 14

mine! Fortunately, there are these ten fundamental principles for maintaining a healthy balance in every aspect of our lives. These ten principles are perhaps the oldest written pattern for life in human history. Many have tried over the years to supplant them, but only to their own personal detriment.

Chapter 15

The person of the Holy Spirit

THE CENTER WEIGHT FOR relational reality or balance is the very presence, through faith, of the Creator God in your heart. It trusts his enabling presence which empowers us to relational reality. Here are some of Jesus,' the Apostle Paul's, and others words about God's Holy Spirit:

> John 14:26: "But the Helper, the Holy Spirit, whom the Father will send in My name, He will teach you all things, and bring to your remembrance all that I said to you.
>
> Acts 2:38: "Peter {said} to them, "Repent, and each of you be baptized in the name of Jesus Christ for the forgiveness of your sins; and you will receive the gift of the Holy Spirit."'
>
> Acts 9:31: "So the church throughout all Judea and Galilee and Samaria enjoyed peace, being built up; and going on in the fear of the Lord and in the comfort of the Holy Spirit, it continued to increase."
>
> Romans 5:5: "and hope does not disappoint, because the love of God has been poured out within our hearts through the Holy Spirit who was given to us."

Chapter 15

1 Corinthians 6:19 "Or do you not know that your body is a temple of the Holy Spirit who is in you, whom you have from God, and that you are not your own?"

2 Timothy 1:14: "Guard, through the Holy Spirit who dwells in us, the treasure which has been entrusted to {you}."

Ignatius was one of the many early Christian leaders martyred for his faith In Jesus Christ. After his conversion to Christianity, he called himself "Theophorus," or "God-Bearer." At his trial, the examiner asked him why he had taken on this new name. He respectfully answered, "Because since I have been born again, I always bear about with me and in me God the Holy Spirit."

To live in relational reality requires us to have the Holy Spirit living in our hearts. We carry the person of the Holy Spirit, who is God, the very God/Creator of all, literally by faith living as another person in our hearts. He is the "center weight" which keeps us balanced.

One is an examination of the essential power of the Holy Spirit. The Creator's presence in our lives and hearts establishes our center weight outside of time. We become creatures connected to and from eternity and for eternity. God's presence in our lives anchors us in his life which transcends time and space. His presence in our life establishes within us genuine, sincere relationships beyond human limitations. The Creator of time has as his primary agenda for us to be a people so emotionally healthy, so stable in our relationships, we will last for eternity.

The most significant issues of life are always relational. It is only with the injection of the weight of the Holy Spirit's presence in our lives that we can fully understand and express his transcending love, acceptance, forgiveness, and grace for all of us. It is his presence which gives balance. He in his fullness brings eternity into our hearts. In his eternity there is no past nor future; it is all present tense. He calls us to live in the present. Now is the only time we can live in relational reality with our Creator and all others. We may want to in the future or we wish we had in the past, but only now can we truly live! All else is wishful thinking.

Relational Reality

Don't misunderstand me. The Creator is ever present; he created time, he is outside of time while with Jesus Christ he established his foothold within time. By our faith, in our hearts, the Creator continually implants his life in time. Bonded together by Jesus' sacrifice, the Creator is vitally invested in your life here and now. This is a reality, not a clever fiction. This is the truth of life which changes everything ultimately for good.

He is using the circumstances of our lives. He is working toward our character transformation. He is molding each of us, individually, into a unique image of the Creator. It is the image of our Creator that only we as an individual can reflect. He is doing this not just for us but for people we love and long to be in a healthy relationship with. He is doing this for the good news that we all can live in relational reality.

Never forget Jesus came to make wrong relationships right, first with our Creator and then with one another. His Holy Spirit's goal is to see each believer come to authentic unique likeness to Jesus Christ—a goal that is often very elusive because it is hidden in outward behaviors of flawed people. Still, this is a work in progress. As we yield our lives to him daily, as we commit to one another in the ten principles of relational reality, as we band together in honest, transparent relationships, his life in us manifests life on a level none outside his relationship can claim.

Chapter 16

Good and evil

AS IN ALL RELATIONSHIPS, good things happen and bad things happen. But usually we define the good and bad of a thing based on subjective fiction rather than objective truth.

Understanding good and evil is both at the same time relatively simple and mighty complex.

First of all, we don't get to decide what good and evil are. Sorry, but we just don't. Good and evil are part of the context of creation.

Here is the plain and the simple part: That which advances the Creator's purpose is good and that which does not is evil. Even if you (in your wrongheadedness, where you deny logic and rational thought) do not understand there is a Creator, your wrongheadedness dictates your concept of right and wrong becoming entirely subjective and thereby eventually self-destructive. Think it through.

Here comes the complicated part: Your view of the Creator will dictate your understanding of good and evil, right and wrong.

If you are an agonistic evolutionist (used to be called being an animist), you will view human life as being no better than any other kind of life. So the taking of a small animal's life to feed a small child is morally equitant to a cannibal eating a small child. Human life is no more valuable than an animal's or plant's. Or you may even believe that human life is destructive to the natural order of things (evil); since all life has the same standing, humans are detrimental to other forms of life, and therefore it is a good thing to reduce the number of humans to bring the nature order (good) into balance. This is also self-destructive; think it through. If this is your belief, then you are the problem, if you are human.

If you are fundamentally a Christian, you believe you been given a great commission to spread Jesus' love, grace, and forgiveness to the world with compassion and charity. The ultimate good is God and his love shown in Jesus. Ultimate evil is the sin (self-centeredness) nature in man, which separates us from God. This has been propagated by Satan, a created being who first chose self-centeredness and spread it to mankind.

If you are fundamentalist Muslim, you believe you have been called to force the world to turn to Alla for the ultimate good so that all people should worship Alla and be righteous. Evil is humans who do not worship Alla as taught by Mohammad.

If you are Buddhist, then good and evil is entirely subjective in a balancing act (the Ying and Yang); one needs the other for the offset of the other. Therefore there is no real objective evil, just half of the whole in a never-ending cycle. Therefore there is no real objective evil, just half of the whole in a never-ending cycle, and when you throw in reincarnation as the way to advance to the next incarnation by doing good it gets confusing, because my good karma by doing good to another may be short-circuiting theirs by not allowing them the suffering for a past life.

We can see even now that one's concept of the Creator determines how you understand good and evil.

As best we can, let's follow the tracks of the Creator to determine some basic concepts and definitions of good and evil. It is easier than you may think.

Good: those behaviors, actions, events, and motivations which result in our reflection or extending of the Creator's purpose.

Evil: those behaviors, actions, events, and motivations which result in our reflection absent of or in contrary to the Creator's purpose.

Chapter 16

The key to understanding good and evil is one's understanding and/or belief in the Creator.

Now let's stop and think about history for a second. We humans (the vast majority) lived basically the same way for thousands of years; some say tens of thousands of years. Think about it, all most everyone grew their own food, lived in rural areas, and avoided crowds to keep from getting hurt or diseased. Most lived very short lives. Life was brutal up until pretty much the mid-nineteenth century. Then it began to change dramatically. Lots of folks have ideas why, but a good argument can be made the United States of America was the driving force for the modernization of the world. But that's a different discussion.

In 150 years humans have gone from living on farms to living in great cities. Then most families were digging in the dirt to raise food, and/or personally butchering animals, wild or domestic, for food. Now we are far removed from that basic understanding of life, that things die so we can live.

We have laid aside the connection of basic living fundamental realities for distracting entertainment.

We have laid aside the personal understanding and experience of individual responsibility which provides the privilege of eating and shelter. We are creating a society which has no anchor or knowledge of good and evil because of the single basic concept which is the foundation for all morality and knowledge.

Being removed from the daily work requirement of the necessities of life has had an impact upon an understanding of reality. The dependence upon the natural forces of the world and that which controls them created in those who lived 150 years ago (and those who still live on farms) an understanding of the fundamentals of life and that which life demands to continue and advance. There is a quote from the movie *Princess Bride* where the Dread Pirate Roberts is speaking to Princess Buttercup: "Life is pain, and anyone who tells you different is trying to sell you something." That is life on this planet up until the last 150 years.

Being removed from this daily work requirement for basic necessities is part of our misunderstanding about the Creator's nature. Reality is the Creator's love and compassionate righteousness and forgiveness wrapped in the harsh concepts of pain, grueling daily work, and routine loss of loved ones.

For full disclosure, I am a Christian. And my understanding of good and evil is consistent with most of Western civilization. From this point on I will be looking at genuine spiritually from my Christian point of view. Don't close the book yet. I think there are arguments here you may not have bumped into yet.

In this time of terrorism dominating the news, there is a lesson we can learn from the primitives who wish to bring about the caliphate. Human pain and suffering, regardless of how brutal or how it is brought about, as long as it has as the goal obedience to the Creator, is a small, timely price to pay for eternal benefits. They fight the good fight according to their understanding of who the Creator is.

We do not agree with this concept in any way, but seeing the application of a seventh-century understanding of religion can help us understand the concepts of judgment, hell, and righteousness from a fundamental point of view: the point of view of the authors of the Bible.

If we, as they did, lived in a world of tremendousl suffering and cruelty, then a concept of the Creator expecting and even requiring stern righteousness (brutality) to bring about behavior which will force consistency with the Creator's will is not so hard to understand. It is even reasonable given the bigger picture of the concept of eternal human potential for harm or good.

Conclusion

Good: those thoughts, emotions, behaviors, actions, and motivations which result in our reflection or extending of the Creator's purpose.

Evil: those thoughts, emotions, behaviors, actions, and motivations which result in our reflection absent of or in contrary to the Creator's purpose.

The Creator's Holy Spirit empowers us to live in relational reality.

Jesus' sacrifice is the Creator's avenue for making wrong relationships right, opening the door for relational reality to become effectual in our lives.

The Creator, God the Father, created each of us as unique creative beings to reflect his love in and for all his creation.

The ten ancient principles (commandments) are the very pattern for beautiful, healthy, meaningful relationships. These are the patterns of encouragement as we band together as reflections of our Creator.

1. There is a Creator who is in relationship with his creation.
2. Anything which distracts or diverts from the objective truth of the Creator has inherited and progressive generational (relationally) negative consequences.
3. Speaking of or treating the objective reality of the Creator causally results in the eroding of the foundation all relationships, intellect, and/or objectively clear thinking.

4. Maintaining relational reality demands setting aside one day a week for building, reinforcing, and/or restoring relationships based in reality.
5. Living humbly with gratitude under parental/honored authority is the foundational objectively internal truth which anchors to reality and is the bridge from emotional/relational immaturity to healthy emotional/relational balance.
6. Individual, relational restoration is always possible. Being the Creator's image, we have in ourselves the capacity to bring relational restoration vs. destruction.
7. Fidelity is the reflection of the Creator in all relationships/marriage. Marriage above all human relationships is most unique. It is the most reflective of the Creator's nature. Where a man and a woman come together as one, bodies are complementary, emotions are complementary, and mental perspective become enhanced.
8. Love's evidence is creation. Personal creativity is our clear reflection of the Creator. When we take that which we did not create or earn we diminish ourselves, reject the nature of the Creator, and refuse to honor and recognize his reflection in others. We deny reality.
9. Discovering the truth of the Creator establishes an objective platform. Developing subjective fictional accounts of reality and spreading them as if they were the objective truth is the verbal attempt to control others by bringing them into your personal fiction.
10. Being absorbed by another's creative results diminishes your own unique creativity and reflection of the Creator's specific objective for your life.

Living in relational reality changes everything for good permanently.

All of creation waits on people (you and I) as individuals to stand in reality and join together in healthy relational reality to reflect the Creator's love, joy, peace, grace, and truth.

Conclusion

Outside of the Creator only subjective fiction guides relationships.

No one has to live this way.

Seek and you shall find. Ask and you shall receive.

www.ingramcontent.com/pod-product-compliance
Lightning Source LLC
Chambersburg PA
CBHW070510090426
42735CB00012B/2723